Feminist Theatre Practice:
A handbook

Feminist Theatre Practice is a practical guide to theatre-making that explores the different ways of representing or 'seeing' gender. Designed to take the reader through the various stages of making feminist theatre – from warming up, through workshopped exploration, to performance – this volume is organised into three clear and instructive parts:

* Women in the workshop
* Dramatic texts, feminist contexts
* Gender and devising projects

Orientated around the classroom/workshop, *Feminist Theatre Practice* encompasses the main elements of feminist theatre, whether practical or theoretical. Topics covered include the body; feminist working practices; the canon; and feminist aesthetics.

Elaine Aston is Senior Lecturer in Theatre Studies at Loughborough University. She is author of *An Introduction to Feminism and Theatre* (Routledge, 1995), and co-author of *Theatre as Sign-System* (Routledge, 1991).

Feminist Theatre Practice:
A handbook

Elaine Aston

London and New York

First published 1999
by Routledge
11 New Fetter Lane, London EC4P 4EE

Simultaneously published in the USA and Canada
by Routledge
29 West 35th Street, New York, NY 10001

Typeset in Bembo by Routledge
Printed and bound in Great Britain by
Biddles Ltd, Guildford and King's Lynn

British Library Cataloguing in Publication Data
A catalogue record for this book is available from the
British Library

Library of Congress Cataloging in Publication Data
Feminist Theatre Practice: A handbook/Elaine Aston.
Includes bibliographical references and index.
1. Feminist theatre. 2. Women in the theatre. 3.
Feminism and theatre.
I. Title.
PN1590.W64A87 1999
98-37217
792'.082–dc21
CIP

£9.99

ISBN 0–415–13924–4 (hbk)
ISBN 0–415–13925–2 (pbk)

Coventry University

Coventry University

For my mother, June Aston

Contents

Illustrations

Plates

Cartoons

Table

Acknowledgements

My teaching career has enabled me to meet so many women practitioners whose creativity has made this volume possible. In particular my thanks go to Cristina Castrillo, Anna Furse, Jill Greenhlagh, Hilary Ramsden and Jude Winter. A warm thank you also to Tanya Myers who looked after my Women and Theatre students in the Spring of 1996.

I should also like to thank Susan Bassnett who first introduced me to the Magdalena Project, and to Gilly Adams and Geddy Aniksdal who revived flagging spirits with their wonderful Performing Words Workshop in February 1998.

I am grateful to those students who have been willing to share their creativity and ideas on the Women and Theatre and the Gender and Devising courses at Loughborough University. In particular, I should like to thank Sandy Ankers, Helen Burgun, Anna Burns, Cara Greczyn, Justine Greene, Adele Greensall, Emma Healey, Lucy Hodgson, Chrissie Kiff, Stephanie Little, Yvonne Mycock, Katie Rice, Rachel Nock, Sam Jevons, Tamzin Richardson, Tina Savage, Penny Thane, Claudia West, Danielle West, Karen Wilson and Rachel Wood.

An especially big thank you to Ali Maclaurin who devised a way for us to make our 'selves' in *Self-ish* and whose photographic and artistic skills make an invaluable contribution to this volume. Thank you also to David Hill, Loughborough University, for permission to use his photographs.

I am grateful to my ever patient family: to my partner Ian, to my daughter Magdalene, and to Daniel who came into the world half-way through the writing of this volume. I need also to express appreciation to Talia Rodgers who was kind enough to wait while manuscript and motherhood worked out competing claims on my time. And finally, a thank you to my mother to whom I dedicate this volume.

Prologue:
Handing on ideas

Gillian Hanna: I remember talking to the women of the Royal
Shakespeare Company at a weekend event which these women
had organised because they were feeling really angry about the
way they were being treated. Juliet Stevenson...and I kept saying to
each other, 'Why isn't there some wonderful organisation whereby
women who've been through all this could get paired up with a
younger woman who could phone them up and say, "This shit has
just done X", and the older woman could reply...'
Mary McCuskcr: Turn to page five of your manual, and look at
diagram six for the pincer movement...
(Monstrous Regiment, 1997: 62)

Picture this: a chain of six women, hands outstretched, passing books
from woman to woman. This was an image created by the six women
devising-performers in the *Portraits of Rossetti* project described in
Chapter 9. It is an image that has remained with me during the
writing of this book, in which I am trying to 'hand on' practical
ideas, which have come largely from working with (mostly) young
women concerned with feminist theatre-making, to up-and-coming
generations of young women, or indeed, to any generation of
women just beginning to discover feminism and feminist theatre-
making. The work I present in this handbook has come from over
two decades of studying and spectating women's contribution to
theatre and from over a decade of finding feminist ways to make
theatre in the academy.
　In Britain and in North America the staffing of theatre studies
courses remains predominantly male, while, on the other hand, drama
degree programmes continue to recruit large populations of female
students. As women tutors with feminist ideas about theatre-making

are few and far between, this increases the need for some sort of practical guide. There are very few, if any, *man*uals to which women can turn. The witty commentary from the women of Monstrous Regiment raises a serious point: the difficulty for women to reach each other and to pass on practical (in all senses of the word) advice in what remains a male-dominated profession and, in terms of staffing at least, academy.

This volume, therefore, is designed as a support system: to help and to advise women students of theatre through the feminist theatre-making process. My primary mode of addressing women is not because I see women's theatrical activity as ultimately separatist and for women-only, but because there simply has not been enough, indeed hardly any, notice taken of women's needs in practical theatre work. When writing, I have assumed that the majority of practitioners–readers who turn to this book will be women – women not as a homogeneous group, but characterised by diversity and difference, whose very sites of difference will allow for further and future diversity in the possibilities of feminist theatre-making.

Nevertheless, I hope that there are ideas here that men can also learn from; ideas that can be taken up in mixed sex groups of students where an awareness of gender means that women will not be disempowered or re-marginalised in theatrical activity. Indeed, some of the case-study examples assume a mixed working group, or offer some suggestions specifically for men involved in performing feminist or woman-centred theatre. In any event, I would hope that men sympathetic to feminist theatre-making would be supportive of this claim to a feminist 'space'.

I remain convinced that a feminist theatre practice can help women to 'see' their lives politically: to raise awareness of oppression and to encourage women's creativity. My work in the theatre academy has been on a very modest scale, involving small groups of women who have shared an interest in creating theatre that challenges their representation in our dominant cultural, theatrical and social systems. As women from these groups move on into the world, and, possibly, into avenues of professional theatre, or other avenues of cultural representation, my hope is that they carry the experience and the vision of a feminist practice with them: into theatre and into the world at large, with a view to connecting, challenging and changing their own lives, and the lives of other women, and of men.

Chapter 1

Introduction:

'Stages' in feminist theory and practice

As an academic discipline, theatre studies involves three key areas of study: history, theory and practice. On both sides of the Atlantic, theatre history has the longest pedagogic 'tradition', while the 1980s explosion of critical theory has, arguably, had the most exciting impact on approaches to plays and performance in both critical and practical modes of study. Practice, however, is the element that distinguishes the discipline from its 'sister' arts, where drama or performance may be studied – in literary, English or cultural studies, for example – but not as a practice-based subject.

In an introduction to feminist theatre, Lizabeth Goodman highlights how, as an academic subject, feminist theatre is 'informed by' a number of disciplines, including, for example, women's studies, media studies or politics, at the same time as it is marginalised 'even within otherwise "liberal" institutions' (Goodman 1996: 20). Goodman further makes a distinction between feminist theatre as an academic area of study and as 'an art from which is performed and shaped primarily in public, outside academic institutions' (*Ibid.*). To situate the practice of feminist theatre as primarily 'outside' of the academy, however, in turn threatens to marginalise what has, since the late 1980s and early 1990s, become one of the most exciting areas of study: feminist theatre practice.

Finding ways of making theatre feminist, or making feminist theatre, has evolved principally (although not exclusively) out of two spheres of activity: feminist critical theory and feminist performance. In an earlier (1970s to early 1980s) phase of feminist theatre, these could be said to be operating more discretely: feminist performance happening outside of the academy in the professional practice/s of women making theatre in the context of the 1970s Women's Liberation Movement; feminist critical theory evolving inside the academy – as I have explained elsewhere, slightly later in the theatre academy, than in 'sister' disciplines such as literary or film studies (see Aston 1995a: 1). By the late 1980s, however, there was an increasing exchange of cultural ideas on theory and practice as professional feminist practice came into the academy (in the form of workshops, performances and talks by practitioners); feminist scholars began to write about and to theorise this work; and, in turn, some feminist playwrights and practitioners became interested in theory. Playwright April de Angelis, for example, describes the women writers' salon hosted in 1990 through the new writing company Paines Plough:

> The salon met once fortnightly at the Paines Plough offices. It was attended by a varied group of women united by a common interest in writing for theatre and aware that a whole canon of difficult but potentially thrilling literary criticism…awaited them and was ready to revolutionise the way they wrote for theatre. Film theory, we reflected, had already got there, so why couldn't we?…
>
> The speakers that visited the group all seemed pleased with the prospect that normal folk outside of the environs of academia wanted to know more of their territory. These varied theories and approaches were out and getting an airing. Why aren't they more widely acknowledged? Because they are complex, difficult? Dangerous? All three, especially the last. Very dangerous and challenging to how we see the world. Contentious, tending to tip the world on its head, not pack-agable under neat ideological labels, these theories felt 'hot'.
>
> (de Angelis and Furse 1991: 27)

In *Upstaging Big Daddy*, the 1993 American anthology of essays devoted to feminist directing in the academy, Sabrina Hamilton argues that 'the art of theater consists of knowing who to steal from' (1993: 133). Since the late 1980s, feminist theatre-making in the academy has been busy 'stealing' from critical theory and professional practice to the point where, in the 1990s, it has emerged as a theoretical field of practice that deserves more attention than it has been given.

Practice, more specifically feminist practice, as taught and experienced in the theatre academy is the subject of this volume. My primary concern is not to identify and to analyse this aspect of feminist theatre studies, but to document practical proposals for its actualisation or realisation: for making it happen. I wish to use this introduction, however, to outline some of the key 'stages' in the evolution of feminist theory and performance as a contextualising background to the practice-based chapters that follow.

Beginnings: objecting to objectification

In the 1970s feminism began to change women's lives. Those women with access to feminist ideas, thinking and publications – mainly white middle-class women – discovered and challenged the male dominance of social, political, cultural and, for our purposes, theatrical systems. In brief, feminism encouraged women towards a political understanding of how they had been either oppressively positioned, or completely left out of, the 'malestream' of social, cultural and political activity.

As women began to demand equal rights with men, agitating specifically on four basic issues (equal pay; equal education and opportunity; twenty-four-hour nurseries; and free contraception and abortion on demand), their protests made use of *agit-prop* techniques in street demonstrations. Feminists made 'spectacles' of themselves to object to how women were objectified in dominant social and cultural systems of representation. For example, feminist protesters at the Miss World beauty contests in the late 1960s and early 1970s staged counter spectacles, by decorating their own bodies with flashing lights attached to clothing at their breasts and crotches, or parading a dummy draped in the symbols of domestic oppression, such as an apron, a stocking, and a shopping bag (see O'Sullivan (1982) for details and illustrations; see Canning (1996: 46) for details of American protests). This kind of early street protest is embryonic of the body-centred critique of gender representation that, subsequently, was to dominate feminist theatre, theory and practice in the 1980s.

Meanwhile, the street theatre beginnings and theatre festivals seeded the desire among feminist practitioners for a more sustained approach to theatre-making. Consequently, feminist practitioners began to set up their own 'spaces', companies in which they could explore women's issues in a more developed way. As mainstream playhouses, and even some of the newly formed left-wing socialist companies, failed to give women an equal platform (either in the hierarchical structures of male-dominated theatre work, or as a dramatic subject), forming a company was one way for women to claim a counter-cultural 'space of their own'. In practice this meant that women had greater control over the organisation, content and style of their theatre work. In consequence, they organised their work democratically and non-hierarchically, in line with the consciousness-raising model of the Women's Liberation Movement, and developed acting styles and aesthetics that would facilitate the ethos of collectivity and collaboration, rather than the cult of bourgeois individualism (see Chapter 2 for further details).

Where mainstream theatre represented women as 'belonging' to men, counter-cultural feminist theatre-making sought to re-present women as subjects in their own right: to move women's issues, experiences and stories centre stage. Women desired to be 'seen' as women and not as a representation of a masculinist imagination. This was explored in many different ways, although principally it involved a greater attention to intra-feminine relations (i.e. relations between women – between mothers and daughters, sisters, lesbian lovers, women friends, etc.) on the one hand, and a demonstration of the potentially damaging consequences of inter-sexual relations (i.e. between men and women – husbands and wives, fathers and daughters, brothers and sisters), on the other.

Objections to realism

To develop counter-cultural practices, feminists needed to be able to understand the formal properties and ideological content/s of dominant cultural forms. In cultural fields concerned especially with image-making – theatre, art, advertising, television or film, for example – feminist critics sought to challenge the ways in which women were 'seen'. In the context of film, Laura Mulvey's groundbreaking essay on 'Visual pleasure and narrative cinema' (1975), drew our attention to the binary, heterosexual polarisation of 'woman as image, man as bearer of the look' (Mulvey 1992 [1975]: 27), in her exploration of what has commonly become known as the male gaze. Although subsequent critiques of Mulvey's proposal, including her own self-critique (see Mulvey 1989), have challenged the oversimplification of the gaze as male (singular), her criticism of the 'active/male and passive/female' mainstream (Hollywood film) conventions of looking and narrative organisation remain important to theorising gender in visual forms of culture.

In theatre, Mulvey's concept of the gaze assisted with an understanding of the ways in which the conventions of the dominant tradition of domestic realism could be seen to uphold an 'active/male and passive/female' structuring of narrative and agency. Although some feminists, both in the academy and in the profession, adopting a bourgeois or liberal feminist position, were prepared to argue for a greater representation of women in the theatrical 'malestream' on 'malestream' terms, others objected to the objectification of women in the realist tradition, and in particular, to the character-based, Method-acting, derived from the teachings of Constantin Stanislavski, attendant upon it. The character roles made available for women to 'get into' in this 'method' invite the actress to identify with the oppression of the female character to whom she has been assigned. As feminist theatre scholar Sue-Ellen Case explains 'the psychological construction of character, using techniques adapted from Stanislavski, placed the female actor within the range of systems that have oppressed her very representation on stage' (Case 1988: 122). Or, as Gillian Hanna, a founding member of the socialist–feminist theatre company, Monstrous Regiment, objected:

> Rarely were we able to play women who lived on stage in their own right. We were always someone's wife, mother or lover. (*Someone* being a man, of course.) Our theatrical identity was usually defined in terms of our relationship to the (more important) male characters. We only had an existence at all because we were attached to a man.... As Mary McCusker was often heard to muse: 'If I have to play another tart with a heart of gold in a PVC skirt, I'm going to throw up.'
>
> (Hanna 1991: xvii)

Feminist playwrights and practitioners who felt alienated by the realist structures of 'women-belonging-to men' wanted to explore other theatrical forms and acting styles to represent their experiences, themes or subjects. It was not so much a question of finding *new* forms, but of *re-working* old or established forms and styles, in the interests of feminist dramatic and stage practice/s. Playwright Caryl Churchill, for example, talked about an awareness of 'the "maleness" of the traditional structure of plays, with conflict and building in a certain way to a climax' (Churchill, quotation in Fitzsimmons 1989: 90). Company members of the lesbian group Siren felt that everything they needed to say, show, communicate could simply not be contained 'in a naturalistic setting or with a narrative that just went beginning, middle, end, or a one-act play', rather, 'what we needed were slicing techniques, ways of suspending belief, to get the imagination and the emotions operating on many different levels' (Siren 1997: 81).

Despite the recent move towards the critical 'rehabilitation' of realism (see Chapter 6), practitioners whose sexual politics are at odds with the heteropatriarchal systems of realist belonging, remain unequivocal about the dangers of realism. To offer a brief example: in *Belle Reprieve*, a collaborative, transgressive queer re-visioning of Tennesse Williams's *A Street Car Named Desire* (produced 1991), Blanche, 'a man in a dress', stops a scene in which the cast are singing and dancing in lantern-costumes. He/she protests 'I can't stand it! I want to be in a real play!' (Bourne, *et al.* 1996: 178). Stanley, played by 'a butch lesbian', takes Blanche back to the 'real play' of *Street Car*. A violent encounter between them ensues. Blanche objects, but Stanley counters: 'If you want to play a woman, the woman in this play gets raped and goes crazy in the end' (p. 181).

Re-figuring the body: cultural–feminist theory and practice

By the late 1980s there was a body of feminist theatre scholarship devoted to re-visioning theatre history, theory and practice. The dramatic syllabus had begun to change as feminists took issue with those 'canonical' texts, written mostly by men, for their representation of women (see Chapter 5), and, also searched for 'lost' works by women buried underneath the male tradition of 'great' literature (see Chapter 6). As Gayle Austin argues in her introduction to *Feminist Theories for Dramatic Criticism*, if we start to notice when women appear as characters and when they do not, then this 'means making some "invisible" mechanisms visible and pointing out, when necessary, that while the emperor has no clothes, the empress had no body' (Austin 1990: 1). Feminist theatre scholarship has drawn our attention to those 'stages' in theatre history when women did not have bodies at all: when the male actor mimed the 'feminine'. Consequently, it is not surprising to find that a principal concern for many feminist practitioners has been the re-appropriation of their own bodies.

The return to the 'female' body or to 'female' culture characterises the feminist position originally termed radical feminism, now more commonly designated cultural feminism. This position sees patriarchy at the heart of inequality between men and women, and addresses oppression by prioritising experiences peculiar to women: birthing, mothering, menstruating, and so on. Radical–feminist performances highlighted the reclaiming of the 'female' body from patriarchal victimisation. Case described how, for example, the 1970s American company It's All Right to be Woman Theatre began 'its productions with a woman touching various parts of her body, reclaiming them from patriarchal colonisation. The troupe and audience would chant, "our faces belong to our bodies, our bodies belong to our lives"' (Case 1988: 66).

Subsequently, however, the essentialist premise of radical–feminist performance has made it the object of much feminist criticism. As lesbian–feminist practitioner and scholar Jill Dolan summarises 'they [cultural–feminist critics and artists] assume that subverting male-dominated theatre practice with a woman-identified model will allow women to look to theatre for accurate reflections of their experience' (Dolan 1988: 83). One of the particular difficulties of the 'woman-identified model' is how to encourage the spectator to 'see' differently. For example, where many of the 1970s women performance artists appeared naked in a reclamation of their bodies, for themselves, and for other women, there was no guarantee that the naked body in this 'woman-identified model' would subvert the sign of the 'feminine' in dominant systems of gender representation. As art historian Griselda Pollock explained: the 'attempt to decolonise the female body, [is] a tendency which walks a tightrope between subversion and reappropriation, and often serves rather to consolidate the potency of signification rather than actually to rupture it' (Pollock 1992 [1977]: 140).

That said, the return to the woman's body as a means of giving 'voice' to experiences repressed by the logocentrism of a patriarchal culture, was an important 'stage' in the evolution of feminist ideas and practice. The theoretical model most commonly identified as cultural feminism is the European 'body' of French feminist theory, represented by Hélène Cixous, Luce Irigaray and Julia Kristeva. Although different from each other in many ways, the work of these women is generally identified with a psychoanalytic, Lacanian exploration of women as 'other' in relation to the symbolic ordering of social and cultural representation and communication. In this model, subjectivity is recognised as problematic for women, who are required to participate linguistically, socially, culturally, etc., in a system that constructs them as marginal and alien. 'No longer wishing to be excluded or no longer content with the function which has always been demanded of us (to maintain, arrange, and perpetuate this sociosymbolic contract as mothers, wives, nurses, doctors, teachers…),' then, as Kristeva explained, the question that arises is 'how can we reveal our place, first as it is bequeathed to us by tradition, and then as we want to transform it?' (Kristeva 1982 [1979]: 41–2).

Cixous's proposal for how women should resist and transform their 'place' as marginalised Other was her call for woman to 'write her self'. Cixous's *écriture féminine*, 'writing said to be feminine', was a call for a '*new insurgent*' writing which would have two inseparable parts:

(a) Individually. By writing herself, woman will return to the body which has been more than confiscated from her, which has been turned into the uncanny stranger on display – the ailing or dead figure, which so often turns out to be the nasty companion, the cause and location of inhibitions. Censor the body and you censor breath and speech at the same time…

(b) An act that will also be marked by women seizing the occasion to speak, hence her shattering entry into history, which has always been based on her suppression. To write and thus to forge for herself the anti-logos weapon. To become at will the taker and the initiator, for her own right, in every symbolic system, in every political process.

Cixous 1981 [1975] : 250)

It was this appeal to the body as the site and practice of *écriture féminine* which made it appear particularly attractive to feminist theatre practice. Indeed, for a moment in the 1980s (however essentialist this may appear in retrospect), it seemed as though the future of our practice might lie in the possibility of staging a 'feminine' language that would 'speak' differently to us as women. Writing specifically about theatre, Cixous proposed a transformation of the stage 'so that a woman's voice could be heard for the first time', further stating that 'if the stage is woman, it will mean ridding this space of theatricality. She will want to be a body-presence; it will therefore be necessary to work at exploding everything that makes for "staginess" ' (Cixous 1984: 547).

Cixous has herself experimented with pieces for theatre. In *Portrait of Dora* (1979) (see Chapter 4), she re-visioned the encounter between Freud and his patient Dora in order to resist the masculinist narrative of the Father and the sadistic positioning of patient (woman) as victim in order that Dora's voice might be heard differently. What is often overlooked, however, is that *Portrait of Dora*, although attributed to Cixous, owes a great deal to its adaptation and direction by the French feminist director Simone Benmussa (for more on this point see Diamond 1989a). Benmussa explains:

> The text…was originally written not for the theatre but for radio. It had no need to bother with technical or practical problems.…Next came the idea of founding an actors' workshop at the Théâtre d'Orsay. I thought it would be interesting to start with a text that was not theatrical, as it would enable us to avoid the habitual theatrical yoke, the yoke that constricts the actors' freedom and forces them to keep on the rails of theatrical 'language'. The text came from 'elsewhere'.
>
> (Benmussa 1979: 10–11)

What is exemplified in the theatrical production of *A Portrait of Dora* is the collaboration between theory (Cixous) and theory–practice (Benmussa). Cixous's *écriture feminine*, embodied in her text from 'elsewhere', provides the framework for helping us to 'see' through the sociosymbolic apparatus of representation, but the theory–practice realisation of this requires the 'authoring' skills of the director/adapter and the body-writing skills of the practitioners. Theoretical ideas about (re)discovering the body need concrete proposals, devices, or registers for their enactment. That said the Cixous–Benmussa example illustrates the possibility of a theorised stage practice that has subsequently become an important model in feminist theatre practice in the academy; working on theoretical texts from 'elsewhere' has become a way of giving direction to feminist practice/s.

'Doubled vision': materialist–feminist practice

For other feminists, re-viewing women's experiences rooted/routed in and through the body was not enough, as this did not pay attention to the material conditions that produce and determine gender, class, race or sexuality. In contrast to the revisionist aims of a body-based cultural–feminist practice, materialist–feminist practice is one which seeks to make a further, arguably more radical, intervention in the apparatus of representation, through the alienation of the gender sign–system. As Dolan explains: 'the pressing issue for feminists becomes how to inscribe a representational space for women that will point out the gender enculturation promoted through the representational frame and that will belie the oppressions of the dominant ideology it perpetuates' (Dolan 1988: 101). The theatrical field of materialist feminism is arguably the most significant, not just in terms of political objectives, but because it is the domain in which a feminist practice has extensively collaborated with theory. In this model, materialist–feminist theorisation of representation combines with a feminist re-visioning of a Brechtian-based, materialist practice.

Teresa de Lauretis has written extensively on systems of representation and the limitations and oppressions of such systems for women. In *Alice Doesn't* (1984), de Lauretis employed a complex methodology rooted in feminism, semiotics, psychoanalysis and cinema, to demonstrate the gap between 'woman', defined as 'a fictional construct, a distillate from diverse but congruent discourses dominant in Western cultures' and 'women', explained as 'the real historical beings who cannot as yet be defined outside of those discursive formations, but whose material existence is nonetheless certain' (de Lauretis 1984: 5). The relation between these two, de Lauretis argued, is 'like all other relations expressed in language…an arbitrary and symbolic one, that is to say, culturally set up' (p. 6). In the introduction to her subsequent influential study *Technologies of Gender* (1987), de Lauretis summarised 'the subject that I see emerging from current writings and debates within feminism is one that is at the same time inside *and* outside the ideology of gender, and conscious of being so, conscious of that twofold pull, of that division, that doubled vision' (1987: 10). De Lauretis demonstrated the constant difficulty for women of being both represented as Woman at the same time as knowing 'that we are not *that*' (*Ibid.*).

In seeking to make visible the 'gap' between the 'real' and the representational in a 'not *that*', resistant style of playing, the feminist performer found a useful ally in the political theatre model of Bertolt Brecht. Brecht's own preoccupations were class- rather than gender-based. His theatre sought to revolutionise an oppressed proletariat, but failed to see gender difference as an issue in the struggle of the working classes. The potential of the Brechtian model for a materialist–feminist practice, comes, therefore, not directly from Brecht, but from the work of feminist scholars and practitioners who have harnessed Brechtian theory and practice to the feminist project.

Revisiting aspects of feminist film theory from a feminist theatre position, Elin Diamond's 1988 essay on 'Brechtian theory/feminist theory' (a seminal reference point for feminist theatre criticism, just as Mulvey's 1975 article (Mulvey 1992 [1975]) was in film studies) drew our attention to the practical ways in which feminist theatre did more than make us aware of the gaze and the way in which women are looked at, it offered the opportunity to make a critical intervention in the structures of looking: 'feminist film theorists, fellow-traveling with psychoanalysis and semiotics, have given us a lot to think about but we, through Brechtian theory, have something to give them: a female body in representation that resists fetishisation and a viable position for the female spectator (Diamond 1997 [1988]: 44). Brecht's theorisation of alienation and his practical suggestions to performers on how to demonstrate systems of social oppression through the medium of performance (as opposed to the 'method' of 'getting into character'), can be brought into play in a feminist theatre context for the specific purpose of alienating gender as a sign-system. The alienation effect can be used to demonstrate gender. As Diamond explains:

> A feminist practice that seeks to expose or mock the strictures of gender, to *reveal* gender-as-appearance, as the effect, not the precondition, of regulatory practices, usually uses some version of the Brechtian A-effect. That is, by alienating (not simply rejecting) iconicity, by foregrounding the expectation of resemblance, the ideology of gender is exposed and thrown back to the spectator.
>
> (Diamond 1997: 46)

A Brechtian-based practice, combined with feminist theorisations of gender, has provided a means of making a materialist intervention into the framing of the 'feminine' (see Chapter 4).

The politics of 'style' and the 'trouble' with gender

There are two final 'stages' I should like to introduce as influential in the evolution of a feminist theatre practice in the academy: the rise of physical theatre and gender theory. Physical theatre is widely practised both inside and outside the theatre academy; gender theory is studied across a range of subject areas. Feminist theatre-making in the academy brings these two elements together to work towards an aesthetics and performance register that challenges the apparatus of representation. Briefly, the background to the practical and critical evolution of these final 'stages' is as follows.

For many professional feminist practitioners the economic squeeze on political theatre in the 1980s was in part responsible for the displacement of issue-based, political theatre and the rise of a theatre which prioritised style over (political) content. As Hanna, looking back over British theatre in the 1980s, commented: 'The '80s [was] the decade of style. What they [small-scale companies] were doing was much more attractive to people in the '80s because it wasn't difficult, it was de-politicised. Nobody was asking any awkward questions about life' (Monstrous Regiment 1997: 65). 'Style', now more commonly designated as 'physical', characterises much of the 1990s small-scale and middle-scale company work on the British stage. As Hanna suggested, most of (but not all of) this company work reflects an interest in style at the expense of politics, although one might argue that at the very least this politicises the logocentricism of play-writing, and of the realist tradition in particular, which has tended to dominate both British and American styles.

While a physical performance register may be used to find imaginative ways of acting out 'classic' scripted plays, more commonly it is associated with and used extensively in the practice of non-scripted devised theatre. Like 'physical theatre', devising is not in itself a political practice, but does offer political possibilities. The co-editors of *Upstaging Big Daddy* argue, for example, that 'constructing [i.e. devising] the text is what you do when you can't bear to direct one more play by Shakespeare, Ibsen, Pinter, or Shaw ' (Donkin and Clement 1993: 151). Or, as Alison Oddey states in *Devising*:

> Devised theatre is a contemporary reflection of culture and society....It is about the relationship of a group of people to their culture, the socio-political, artistic and economic climate, as well as issues or events surrounding them....Choice, opportunity and infinite possibility set devised theatre apart from conventional play text production.
>
> (Oddey 1994: 23)

Given women's relationship to culture and their representation in the 'conventional play text', it is hardly surprising that they have preferred to create their own performances. Devising offers women a way of making theatre that means that they do not have to work on a 'big daddy' script – or, if constrained to do so, may assist in making a radical intervention in a 'canonical' or 'conventional play text' (see Chapter 5). As a process, this offers women the opportunity to practise theatre collaboratively and democratically (see Chapter 2). Many of the plays created by feminist companies in the late 1970s, for example, were devised collaboratively, rather than scripted by a playwright. Productions by the Women's Theatre Group between 1974 and 1978, for instance, were all devised by the company. What distinguished this model of feminist devising, however, from the more recent, corporeally based model, was its concentration on feminist issues. Issue-based devising focused on what women wanted to say, rather than on the style in which they wished to 'say' it.

Devising physically, on the other hand, is significant for women who perform, because they first, as Cixous suggested in her manifesto, have to find their bodies (see Chapter 3). As Jude Winter, devising-performer of Dorothy Talk theatre company observed: 'When I see mixed companies the male performers in physical theatre shows are often very strong. And I look at the women performers and I ask myself, 'Why aren't they as good?'' (Ramsden and Winter 1994: 122–3). Women may, as Winter's comments went on to suggest, need more nurturing and support to perform in a physical register, but arguably, they have more to gain through 'undoing' the social, cultural and theatrical conditioning of their bodies. Most important of all, they have greater control over both the content and the form of their theatre work.

The devising-performer is by no means exclusive to a feminist stage practice. She/he figures in a variety of companies with a focus on the body as agent and corporeal 'text', companies who, as Hanna observed, are not necessarily political. What distinguishes the devising-performer in feminist theatre-making, however, is her re-framing of gender through cultural–feminist and materialist–feminist performance registers.

Despite the centrality of the live body to theatre through which it acts out or makes visible its concerns, or in the case of feminist theatre, specifically, the focus on the body as si[gh]te of gender representation, rather curiously, as Gayle Austin notes, this sphere of feminist activity has been, and continues to be, overlooked by women's studies: 'women comfortable with the idea of interdisciplinary work still shy away from using dramatic texts' (Austin 1990: 2). More recently, the exclusion of drama and theatre from critical and theoretical gender study has entered a new phase. The 'trouble' with some gender theory, and here I am alluding to Judith Butler's influential study *Gender Trouble* (1990), and its sequel *Bodies that Matter* (1993), has been its displacement of the live body and performance by the concept of gender, 'performativity', and the domain of theory as the written. In trying to re-direct misreadings of *Gender Trouble*, specifically the concept of a 'choosing subject', one who decides her gender (Butler 1993: x), Butler writes out/off the possibilities of performance because, as Diamond explains, 'the performer, implies one who ontologically precedes and then fabricates gender effects' (Diamond 1997: 46). In Butler's own words:

> in no sense can it be concluded that the part of gender that is performed is therefore the 'truth' of gender; performance as bounded 'act' is distinguished from performativity insofar as the latter consists of a reiteration of norms which precede, constrain, and exceed the performer and in that sense cannot be taken as the fabrication of the performer's 'will' or 'choice'.
>
> (Butler 1993: 234)

To reject performance, however, is to close down the possibility of a field of theory which, in a feminist domain, can at least show us partial gender 'truths'. Performing 'performing-ness' can show the ways in which gender is played out through a 'reiteration of norms', thereby allowing us to contest it. Or, to use de Lauretis's model, it allows us the possibility of demonstrating, 'but I am not that'. As a resistant mode of 'doing' rather than 'writing' it offers the possibility of new 'ways of seeing'.

Sphere of 'disturbance': towards a feminist practice

It is within this matrix of feminist theory, gender theory and feminist performance that a feminist practice in the academy began to emerge. In the 1980s, once feminism had begun to make itself felt in the theatre academy, the dramatic syllabus began to change. Increased access to feminist plays (see Chapter 7) meant that it was no longer necessary for large groups of predominantly female students to try to make practical (and ideological sense) of plays written by predominantly (although not exclusively) white, heterosexual, middle-class men. Or if they did, they could use feminist criticism and theory to challenge such plays and the ways in which they are performed and staged, and, in turn, stage them differently (see Chapter 5).

As professional feminist practitioners came into the academy to workshop and to perform, it meant that women studying theatre were introduced to techniques for either performing feminist scripts (see Chapter 7), or devising their own (see Part 3). Despite the mid-1980s drive towards the possibility of a 'feminine' language for the stage, rooted in cultural–feminist thinking and practice, it became apparent that there was no one way of making feminist theatre, or making theatre feminist. The plurality of workshop practices brought into the academy by professional women practitioners demonstrated a range of approaches, techniques and methods, dependent upon individual theatrical, personal, political, geographical and feminist histories. However, such workshopping did share some common ground in its diversity: it differed from conventional pedagogic practice through the acknowledgement that cultural and material factors such as gender, race, class, age and sexuality might make a difference to theatre work – methodologically, stylistically, thematically and aesthetically.

More recently, in the 1990s, the impact of devising and working physically, combined with feminist and gender theories has encouraged us towards a theoretically informed style of feminist practice where the body/voice of the devising-performer is the site of a critical engagement with the gender politics or representation. In contradistinction to gender theory à la Butler, located in the textual, the written, feminist theatre practice articulates its concerns through 'doing'. To continue to marginalise this work is to overlook the possibility of a field of theorised activity that ends, begins and processes through real bodies that 'matter' very much.

While it is important to stress that there is no one way of practising feminist theatre, it is useful to have some broad-based conceptualisation of feminist aims and objectives in the theatre workshop. As your own practice evolves, you can define these for yourselves. My own proposals, which underpin and inform the practice-based chapters that follow are:

- That a feminist practice may constitute a theoretical domain.
- That a feminist practice may operate formally and ideologically as a 'sphere of disturbance'.
- That feminist practice 'steals' from wherever and whatever is necessary to create the desired 'disturbance'.

- That representational systems (of gender, sexuality, class, race, etc.) are the subject (and are subjected to) this 'disturbance'.

To elaborate: throughout this volume feminist critical theory 'directs' or orientates many of the proposals for feminist theatre practice that may in turn (re)-'direct' theory. That said, it is essential to stress that a feminist practice does not follow a predetermined set of rules; it is not designed to 'fit' a 'theory'. Abstract ideas, theoretical proposals developed and explored through practice constitutes a process of endless beginnings, discoveries, unforeseens, contradictions and, inevitably, confusions. What guides us through this in a feminist theory–practice context is our commitment to exploring different ways of representing or 'seeing' gender; of making ourselves visible when we cannot be 'seen' in dominant systems of social, cultural and theatrical representation.

The 'sphere of disturbance' is a concept that I have 'stolen' from Simone Benmussa's notes in *Benmussa Directs* (1979) (see earlier on Cixous and Benmussa). As a director Benmussa attempts to define her task as working 'within the sphere of…"disturbance", in which escape from their original meaning to the point of becoming indistinguishable from each other' (Benmussa 1979: 20–1). She explains how she deploys 'disturbance', 'in its active, mobile sense, to oppose it to stagnant categories' (p. 21). Taking my cue from Benmussa's notes, I wish to argue a feminist theatre practice as a 'sphere of…'disturbance'. It is not to be categorised as one type or style of theatre, as a 'theatre of the body', as 'visual theatre', as aural, physical or devised theatre, but as a practice that 'steals' or draws on whatever is necessary, from wherever it is needed, to oppose categorisation; to disturb the processes that en-gender meaning and representation; to activate a sphere of doing for the purpose of 'undoing'.

That which a feminist theatre practice seeks to disturb are our systems of representation that refuse women the possibility of representing themselves; refuses them agency, subjectivity, identity and so on. Gender may therefore be the subject, or be subjected to critical scrutiny and transformation through workshopping and performance processes.

The project

To keep practice as the focus of this volume, I have tried, beyond this introductory chapter, not to overshadow practical suggestions with theoretical explanations. At the same time, I acknowledge that those practitioners–readers who are new to this field will find theoretical explanations both useful and necessary, and I have, therefore, included a Glossary to help explain the political and theoretical terms of feminist reference used in the volume. The second part of the Glossary offers brief contextualising notes to practitioners – performers, writers and companies – whose woman-centred, feminist or gender-aware theatre-making is referenced in the volume, but again may be new to some readers. Where appropriate, I have also tried to include practical 'voices' in the form of sound bites, which I hope will be useful to orientate ideas and practical suggestions, and to indicate the many feminist 'sources' and influences that inform this study. The 'resources sections' accompanying each chapter are designed to help with materials for resourcing further work, and offer theoretical and practical suggestions as appropriate.

The chapters that follow are designed to take you through different spheres of theatre-making, beginning in Part I with an introduction to the principles of feminist organisation (Chapter 2); 'undoing' the social and cultural thinking about our bodies as preparation for theatre work (Chapter 3); and sketching preliminary workshop ideas and techniques for 'disturbing' gender (Chapter 4).

Part II concentrates on scripted work, and includes practical suggestions for working on and in 'canonical' texts and contexts (Chapter 5); for exploring what happens when the feminist performer confronts realism (Chapter 6); and finding feminist performance registers for feminist scripts (Chapter 7). Part III is devoted to feminist devising projects, and all three chapters here offer guidelines and case studies of a practice which, as the title to the final chapter, 'Performing your selves', suggests, highlight the performer as the principal agent and creator of the text.

In the interests of lucidity, I have organised the work into this tripartite structure, but the practitioner–reader should aim to extract exercises and ideas according to practical needs. My proposal is that these suggestions should combine and re-combine across parts and chapters into further possibilities of practice.

Part I

Women in the workshop

All three chapters in Part I are in some way concerned with women in the workshop. Chapter 2 offers details about how to start thinking about feminism and about the feminist principles of democratic theatre-making; the sharing of roles and the distribution of responsibilities. Chapter 3 collects together ideas about how to begin to relax, to concentrate and to work physically and vocally. Chapter 4 details practical ideas for workshops focusing on gender.

The demands of writing dictate that, ultimately, there has to be an order to parts, chapters, sections, sentences, words and so on. In writing I am forced into linear structures. I have to organise my ideas – but I know I could have organised them differently; presented them in a different 'order'. In practice, in the workshop, you have the freedom to make different 'orders', different beginnings. Where you begin will depend on your needs and your points of departure. A group of performers or non-performers wanting to focus specifically on gender might begin with the last chapter in this Part, Chapter 4. An experienced group of performers wanting to work together as a group of women for the first time might start with the suggestions about roles and organisation of work in Chapter 2. So begin where you need to – which might even be at the end of the book – and combine any exercises from any of the chapters that are helpful to your feminist theatre-making.

Chapter 2

Feminist directions

In this second chapter I wish to offer guidelines on how you might establish a group to work on feminist theatre projects, and on the possible organisation of roles and the division of labour in a group structure. In setting out these guidelines I refer you to the history of feminist companies whose principle of non-hierarchical sharing 'directs' so much of our contemporary, experimental, collaborative theatre-making.

Forming a women's group

> In the beginning we had a strong sense of wanting to create a space for women in which they could have a go at doing drama in a safe environment. It was important to signal our focus on women. Men don't have to flag up men's theatre because theatre is that anyway.
>
> (Women and Theatre, 1997: 138)

In the feminist climate of the 1970s women felt the need for a 'space' of their own in which to share experiences, feelings and problems that could not be expressed or were not considered important enough to be voiced in a mixed social or cultural context. In the wake of the Liberation Movement, therefore, women organised their own consciousness-raising (CR) discussion groups to give themselves a voice:

> The first task of CR groups was to provide women with a voice. After centuries of silence, CR groups provided a situation in which women could begin to articulate what it felt like to be a

woman. The all-woman composition of the groups provided safety from the scrutiny and criticism of men and gave women an opportunity to enter into a dialogue with other women.

(Case 1988: 65)

In theatre, women set up feminist companies to make a 'space' for their creativity and feminism, which was a low priority in mixed companies – even socialist ones. For example, from its inception in the mid-1970s the Women's Theatre Group (WTG) operated a women-only company policy. Monstrous Regiment started out with (a minority of) men but over time moved to a women-only composition:

> We realised that we had never worked in an all-women, as opposed to women-dominated, environment and we wanted to explore that. We found that it gave us a different kind of freedom to anything we had experienced before and we enjoyed it.

(Hanna 1991: lxii)

Working as a women-only group was a choice which many of the professional feminist companies in the 1970s exercised, because it offered a way for women to gain confidence both about themselves and about their creativity. As an actress explained to Ros Franey in a report on 'Women in the Workshop' for Plays and Players:

> Many women find it difficult to express themselves as individuals with men around, either because they are nervous of men or because they're conditioned to a series of responses whenever a man confronts them. One girl who came to the workshop said it had never previously occurred to her that she had any right to a life unrelated either to her husband or her home.

(Franey 1973: 27)

Many of the pioneering 1970s feminist companies ceased operations in the late 1980s or early 1990s, although the need for women to connect with other women, theatrically and politically, has remained. Although there are far fewer women's companies now than in the 1970s, groups of women still come together, welcoming the 'space' to investigate their creativity as women. Foursight Theatre, for instance, were motivated by the desire to explore what their group had to offer creatively by working as a group of women. Founded in 1987,

Foursight have since used their company of women to concentrate on dramatising women's biography (see Chapter 9).

To offer one final brief example: in the mid-1980s Jill Greenhalgh organised an international festival of women's work in Cardiff, Wales, which brought together practitioners from different countries, cultures and theatre groups. The experience of the festival made women aware 'that for too long they had been complying with their directors to create a male art and not an art which reflected their experience' (Greenhalgh 1992: 108). Out of the energy that came from these women being together came the Magdalena Project, offering regular opportunities for women to meet and to work together internationally:

> Magdalena meetings have offered…women a unique opportunity to meet and share their experiences. Sometimes those meetings have functioned as a support group, as a consciousness-raising group or as a forum where conflicting opinions can be voiced among women, but always as a focal point for women sharing a common interest. Time and again comments from participants have stressed the rarity of such encounters and the value of having them.
>
> (Bassnett 1989: 127)

Your group may wish to begin by having pre-session CR-style meetings, creating the opportunity for women to share both their personal and their theatrical experiences. You may need to meet and to discuss whether you wish to work as a women-only group, or as a mixed group with a majority of women (like Monstrous Regiment in its early days, for example). Discuss:

* Whether working in a women-only context might offer you the opportunity for confidence-building (in the absence of men), and for prioritising your creativity and experience as women.
* Whether gaining confidence in yourself and in your ideas in a women-only space may help to renew energies and to develop new skills for taking back to work in a mixed company.

You may find that the backlash against feminism makes many women suspicious of or hostile to the idea of working in a women-only context, and that the myth of the women's workshop as some sort of bare-your-soul-man-hating-forum is hard to dispel. Try to confront this prejudice early on. Organise preliminary meetings of women who are interested in working together to discuss the apprehensions and possible pleasures of working as a women-only group. Try and maximise the opportunity for women to begin to get to know one another and to find out more about each other. Early CR groups tended to focus on women as one group, rather than looking at factors such as race, class, age, sexuality and so on (Case 1988: 65). Have an informal discussion where you find out more about these differences within a potential group.

Or, if you are thinking of working as a group with a majority of women and minority of men, then you could discuss how you are going to organise the work of the company along gender lines. A recurrent problem in this context is that too much time is spent worrying about whether the men are at ease in the group: women often worry about the men; men often need to be made to feel special for agreeing to work on a women's project. All of this is at the expense of women's theatre work. Consider these reflections by Monstrous Regiment on this issue:

> In effect, we spent a lot of time making sure that the men felt comfortable, and falling head-first into the trap of mothering them....Not that the men found it an easy situation to be in. We were asking them to abandon the privileges of patriarchy and work side by side with women as equals. But the equality was blurred, in that it was informally clear that the women led and directed the company. Perhaps if we had been able to find a different organisational structure, things might have been easier; a structure in which women were formally recognised as being the leaders, having the power; in which the men were employed by the women.
>
> (Hanna 1991: xxx)

A mixed group is less likely to get into difficulty if it discusses the roles of men and women in the organisational structure before project work is underway.

Feminism and feminist sketches

When women first met in CR groups in the 1970s feminism was what brought them together. While this may have had a (falsely) homogenising effect (concealing rather than exposing differences), feminism was the common meeting ground for women. For women who were part of the 1970s movement, or who grew up in its wake, feminism is a given. For younger generations of women who grew up in the Thatcher or Reagan years, knowing only one kind of (right-wing) government, this is not the case. To younger generations, feminism may feel like something that happened before they were born and does not connect with their lives. If your group has a wide age range, it is likely to have a range of feminist or non-feminist experiences to share.

Groups comprised mainly or exclusively of younger women may want to organise initial meetings for politicising the group at the outset. Thrashing out views on feminism, including anti-feminist ones, is a useful way of seeing who may wish to work together. The editors of Aurora Metro's *The Women Writers' Handbook* explain how unresolved conflicts in a writers' workshop can lead to a group falling apart later:

> Conflicts may arise, for example, between specifically feminist women, attending a women's group for political reasons, and women who may be alienated by such views. In some cases, it may be necessary to make a choice, and this involves prioritising who the class is for.
>
> (Robson *et al.* 1990: 22)

Rather than allowing painful group conflicts to disrupt and impede work further on into the making process, try and organise a discussion of feminism as part of your group formation. Brainstorming different views on feminist positions (bourgeois, cultural and materialist feminisms), getting each member of your group to say how they feel about feminism, and to come up with a working definition, and so on, will help you to see whether you have extremes that need addressing at the outset.

Sketches

If you wish to organise a preliminary workshop for finding out about feminism, one way of doing this is to try short *agit-prop* performances. Feminist theatre has a strong tradition of protest theatre. In the suffrage campaign for women's rights at the turn-of-the-century, rallies and demonstrations demanding the vote used sketches to make a political point (see Gardner 1985).

Hold a workshop where women in the group are invited to brain-storm experiences of oppression. Try brainstorming ideas on paper in which the women either write a sentence or two about an experi-ence or draw a quick image representative of an experience. The group need a moment to have a look at these ideas and then each woman in turn could narrate her experience to the group. Your group could split into smaller groups to devise sketches for each story. Try and organise yourselves so that you work on a story that did not originate from a woman in your group. Critical distance from the emotional experience will help you with (Brechtian) demonstrating and politicising. You might work up sketches that are presented in your working space, or you might make them site-specific. For example, you might stage a sketch about body image in front of the washbasins and mirrors in a female cloakroom, or in a women's clothing section in a local department store.

When all of the sketches have been staged, meet together as one large group to review what areas of oppression and feminist issues emerged. Are there common areas of oppression in your group, or are experiences very different (perhaps pointing to a diversity of factors in the group – age, race, or class, for example)? The woman whose story has been acted out could be invited to comment on what happened to her personal experience in the political sketch. How does she feel? What does she see differently?

See if it is possible to use your sketches to agree on a working definition of feminism, which you can use as a reference point as you work. Pin it up in your space so that the group can refer back to it in moments of doubt, difficulty or confusion.

Organisation

When you have agreed on your group composition and held prelim-inary discussions about feminism, you need to think about establishing a working structure. Most mainstream theatre is hierar-chically organised with writers and directors making the 'big' decisions, and actors and technicians acting them out. A legacy of the alternative political and feminist companies of the 1970s, however, is the principle of democratic organisation. Groups such as WTG or the mixed, ensemble, new writing company Joint Stock began by encouraging all members to have an equal share in the making processes. Feminist critic Michelene Wandor, writing on Joint Stock's

working method for Caryl Churchill's *Cloud Nine*, a play about
sexual politics, explained:

> The desire to democratise the play-producing process springs
> from a political opposition to the traditional, hierarchy-conscious
> theatre, where individual skills are so fetishised that myths
> develop: writers are temperamental flowers, actors are intellectual
> zombies, directors are martinets. Political and alternative theatre
> challenges the crudities of these myths, by finding ways to
> encourage responsibility for all stages of the work: for what a
> play is saying as well as how it is saying it; a politicising of the
> whole aesthetic process.
>
> (Wandor 1979: 14)

Given the ways in which women occupied and, despite legislation,
still occupy, an unequal position in social, familial, cultural and
theatrical structures, the principle of non-hierarchical, democratic
organisation was fundamental to feminism and to the organisational
and aesthetic principles of feminist theatre-making.

I Iowever, while companies, such as WTG, began by insisting on
collective decision-making and organisation, they moved gradually
towards a structure that combined democracy with skills specialisa-
tion. In practice, for example, this meant that each woman might
have something to say about the design, but one woman would take
on overall responsibility for this area of theatre work. On the other
hand, it might also mean that a woman without a skill in design or in
writing could ask the group to support and to encourage her in
acquiring this skill. Again, many feminist companies found that an
all-women group gave them a greater degree of security, support and
confidence for nurturing skills, than in a mixed company.

You can think about all three of these possible directions when
organising your work:

* Collective organisation in which all members have an equal
  share in every task.
* Collaboration with an emphasis on skills specific to individual
  members.
* Collaboration with an emphasis on individual skills development
  and acquisition.

The sections that follow provide further introductions about how to think about sharing the tasks of research, writing, directing, performing and designing.

Dramaturg

The professional role of dramaturg is more commonly recognised in the USA and European countries outside of Britain. The role and duties assigned to the professional dramaturg will vary from country to country. It is not possible, therefore, to offer a general job description of the dramaturg, rather, her role needs to be context-defined. In feminist theatre-making a possible job description for a dramaturg is feminist researcher. The kinds of feminist research tasks that your dramaturg/s might undertake are as follows.

Feminist research: general

The kind of research that you undertake will, of course, vary from project to project. Research is as wide-ranging as the choice of project. You may find you need to go out to talk to specific communities of women about a particular issue, or you may need library searches for documents about a feminist subject. Your dramaturg can take overall responsibility for the organisation of research. In a collective model this may mean co-ordinating research undertaken by all group members. Or, the role of the dramaturg may be organised so that she takes primary responsibility for bringing materials to your group to share and to workshop.

When researching, remember to keep thinking theatrically. Try not to think of your feminist research as an academic task that you have to get out of the way before you can get on with the business of performance, but as integral and fundamental to your performance work. It is a good idea for research materials to be circulated early in the group, not just for shared discussion, but for beginning work-shopping.

Feminist theory

Project work discussed in this volume is, directly or indirectly, informed by feminist critical theory. The dramaturg may be the person whom the group invites to undertake theoretical research that can be shared. Remember to encourage all members of your group to share in theoretical understandings. A project where a group has

decided to work with French feminist theory, but only one woman
has heard of or read about Hélène Cixous is almost certain to get
into difficulty. When working with theory, your dramaturg could be
invited to bring seminal writings to a group so that everyone can
work on them. She could be asked to select material: to choose
extracts, rather than a whole book, to provide a list of key ideas and
associated reading, and so on, but it is important that everyone partic-
ipates in the dissemination of theoretical ideas.

Feminist drama and theatre

Your dramaturg could be invited to find one or two feminist plays
relevant to the project you are working on. Looking at published
examples of work from women writers or companies may often
inspire your group to see how, or how not, they would like to treat a
similar subject. Also, your dramaturg could check to see which feminist theatre is currently being performed. If there are performances
that you feel may be relevant, then all of your group could go to see
them. If one woman misses a performance that inspires the rest of the
group, again, your work is likely to be disadvantaged.

Assisting and keeping a record

As practical work progresses you may find you need to bring in more
research materials, and your dramaturg may find herself assisting the
director/s and writer/s (see later) by finding materials and offering
practical suggestions about how to work with them. As your group
workshops and devises material it is always useful to keep a record of
exercises, material and ideas generated. Each group member should
be encouraged to keep her own individual records. Additionally, the
dramaturg is well-placed to keep a central record for the group.
Remember, making brief notes will save time and argument over
half-remembered ideas. The central record of devising notes may in
turn take your dramaturg into the sphere of scripting (see later). In
group work the blurring of boundaries between devising and
scripting often happens. As a group, always check that everyone is
happy with any 'blurring' and no one woman is becoming overbur-
dened in the process.

Publicity programme notes

If your group is aiming for a production, rather than a workshopped presentation, and wishes to organise publicity and programmes, the dramaturg is well placed to provide materials for publicity. During her research, for example, she may have come across visual materials suitable for making posters, or have found quotations that a group might be able to include in a programme. Design and execution of publicity may be assigned to another group member, but a dramaturg will be able to save your group time by having research materials to hand.

Writer

Although feminist theatre companies were concerned to operate as democratically as possible, one task that groups felt was especially difficult to organise collectively was the task of writing. Monstrous Regiment, for instance, supported a non-hierarchical organisational structure, but felt that they needed to bring in women writers for scripting. Hanna explains:

> Why should the writer be God? Wouldn't it be more democratic to write scripts collectively? If you were working in a collective, how could one voice represent the ideas of the whole? We acknowledged some truth in this, but there were some areas where we recognised it a bunk. Enough of us (and I was one of them) had been through the painful experience of writing shows collectively in other groups to know that the skill of playwriting was one skill we wanted to acknowledge.
>
> (Hanna 1991: xxxiii)

Finding ways to collaborate with writers was not uncommon in feminist companies: Monstrous Regiment collaborated with Caryl Churchill on *Vinegar Tom* and with Bryony Lavery on *Calamity Jane*. Alternatively, feminist groups also offered women the opportunity to emerge as writer: Tasha Fairbanks of Siren developed her dramatic skills over the company's ten-year history to emerge as the writer in the group, as did Clair Chapman in Spare Tyre.

In brief, your group will need to think about ways in which to organise the task of writing. Three possible models to consider are:

1   Writer and group.
2   Collective writing.
3   Writer emerging from group.

We can look at each of these three models to try to think about the potential pleasures and pitfalls. Thoughts on each model are accompanied by reflections from writers and practitioners – sound-bites to help you with your deliberations.

Writer and group

It may be that a group of women is approached by a woman who identifies herself as a writer – possibly someone who has taken a playwriting course and is keen to develop her skills in this direction. However, you need to be careful about the relationship of the writer to the group. It is all too easy to revert to a hierarchical relationship, which gives priority to the role of the writer and leaves the group outside the working processes. Dramatists and companies who have benefited from collaborative writing experiences, are those who have positively encouraged collaboration in the making processes. Consider this reflection by Caryl Churchill after working on *Vinegar Tom* for Monstrous Regiment:

> I met the whole company to talk about working with them. They gave me a list of books they had read and invited me to a rehearsal of *Scum*. I left the meeting exhilarated. I'd been writing plays for eighteen years, half my life....All this work had been completely solitary – I never discussed my ideas while I was writing or showed anyone anything earlier than a final polished draft. So this was a new way of working, which was one of its attractions.
>
> (Churchill 1982: 39)

On the other hand, Monstrous Regiment had very unhappy and angry reactions from the co-writers of *Scum* – Claire Luckham and Chris Bond – after seeing 'their' play in performance. Luckham and Bond argued that in their view they had been 'commissioned to write a play', not a 'working script', which was why they were angry when they saw the changes to their work (see Hanna 1991: xxxv). Ultimately, Hanna argues that in looking for 'a collective relationship with the writer', the company learnt that there was no 'recipe for what that relationship might be' (p. xxxiii). In other words, there is no way of guaranteeing a successful writer–group collaboration.

However, possibly the most important step to take in trying to work towards a successful collaboration is to make sure that the ethos of collaboration has been understood by both the writer and your group; that both sides feel they are able to contribute. On the part of the writer, this means, as Churchill's comments indicate, no longer working in isolation, and being able to accommodate suggestions from the group. On the part of the group, it means accepting that while they can 'flesh' out, advise on or contribute through work-shopping to a script, the writer may, ultimately, be the person who takes responsibility for the 'backbone' of the script.

Try and agree on a model of collaboration at the start of a project, and if, as you work, you sense this is changing, or needs to change, then try to discuss and agree changes, or compromises, in order to avoid disputes.

Collective writing

This is probably the hardest model to opt for. Trying to involve every woman equally in the writing process is likely to prove time-consuming and unwieldy. Attempting to arrive at a 'script' that everyone is writing is an almost impossible task, even where a group has very good dynamics and gets on well together. That said, here is a relatively positive account from Mica Nava, outlining how WTG's *My Mother Says I Never Should* was written by the group in 1974:

> Having decided on the general issues that we wanted to raise, we did a lot of research: we talked to girls, teachers and parents…we studied contraceptive techniques and the dissemination of advice to young people. Then we pooled our information, created characters and a plot, improvised, and finally went off in twos and threes to write and rewrite. Writing was a long and often painful business, inevitably there were disagreements and compromises, but we also gave each other confidence and took greater risks. Ultimately we felt that the group process distilled a clarity not obtainable by us individually.
>
> (Nava 1980: 115)

Scripting workshopped material in splinter groups of twos and threes is probably a good suggestion in this collective model. However, try and ensure that splinter groups come back to main group meetings with everyone present, in order for material not to become fragmented and disjointed. You need to ensure that each group member has (1) a responsibility for making a specific contribution to scripting; and (2) an understanding of how their specific tasks relates to the project overall. You will also need to find a way of agreeing on who has the final say in what goes into or is left out of a script, which it is almost impossible to do collectively.

Writer in the group

Assigning one woman, who may also be the dramaturg, or the director, or possibly even both, to the role of writer in collaboration with the group, is likely to prove a more productive route – both organisationally and creatively – than collective writing. As is the case of a writer coming into a group, a writer emerging from within the group needs to see her role as a collaborative one: as the central co-ordinator of ideas generated by the group. She will inevitably need time on her own for developing and writing up ideas workshopped by the group, but, as in the situation when a writer joins a group, she should not become an outsider.

In this extract, Clair Chapman, who emerged as the writer for Spare Tyre, discusses the writing processes for the company's 1982 show, *On the Shelf* :

> For *On the Shelf* I kept coming up with lots of material and brought it in to the group. So we had this wealth of material. It wasn't a very satisfactory way to write, really, because at the time I found it hard to take criticism. I went to Susie Orbach for advice, and said, 'I want to write a play but I'm in this collective group.' And she said, 'Write the play, people write plays everyday – write it.' So I wrote it, but this method still felt problematic in terms of writing for the group, rather than as an individual.
>
> This is something we've gradually resolved. What's happened since with the writing is that I've taken control of the structure, the other two [group members] contribute within that. That seems to suit us all and we've put together better plays working this way – plays that actually have a beginning, a middle, and an end. Often, when you go to see shows which have been group-devised, you can tell the group tensions by the way the play is

written. So we've actually arrived at a framework which over-
comes this problem and suits us.

(Spare Tyre 1997: 113)

Performer

> I am an actress. Theoretically the problem of text and dramaturgy
> shouldn't concern me. As an actress my task is to interpret a role, a
> character or to create a character proposing acting materials to a
> director who will use them for a performance. But what would
> happen if the actress were to have an 'idea'? If she didn't accept to
> be simply the interpreter or the performer of a theme chosen by
> the author or the director, but wants to face an issue she has at
> heart?
>
> (Ricciardelli 1992:3)

> I have always felt the difficulty of having to play a character that
> someone's written for me and that I have not been able to create
> myself. No matter how much we talk about a story and a plot, to
> have a character sketched out and given lines, ways, and relation-
> ships that haven't been created by myself – that has always been an
> imposition.
>
> (Winter in Siren 1997: 86)

Actors and actresses employed in mainstream theatre work are most
commonly employed for a role in a play, provided by a writer, and
are closely directed by a single person. On the other hand, feminist
theatre work has moved away from the hierarchisation of performers
in a star-system. Brechtian influences have fostered techniques of
multi-role playing, of emphasising the community of players rather
than the individual player. The emphasis on the group rather than the
individual, on multi- rather than singular role playing or sharing, have
been important to feminist explorations of identity, and subjectivity –
all of which may require some explanation and negotiation in your
group if this appears to be a new way of working.

   Collaborative models of theatre-making may demand a period of
workshopping from the performer in which she/he is required to
generate ideas that are taken up in scripting. For example, working
collaboratively with Caryl Churchill on Joint Stock projects, director
Max Stafford-Clark commented:

Actors are often in a situation where they make the most of what they've got. Their creativity is rarely called upon. You gain their commitment if you say to them: 'The script will finally be written by the author, but first we all have an opportunity to explore our own obsessions and create things from scratch, to explore, to initiate subjects.' You're tapping a source of energy that normally plays don't demand. The workshop is an explo ration and sharing of ideas which, at its best, gives everyone a chance.

(Stafford-Clark, quoted in R. Hayman, *Sunday Times Magazine*, 2 March 1980, p. 27)

Input will of course vary according to how you are organising different creative tasks in your group. However, the performer may be invited to contribute to the creative, intellectual and aesthetic processes of the theatre work, in the following kinds of ways:

• She brings her feminism to the project.
• She may be invited to create her own characters and situations, or to help with authoring a scene.
• She may author material out of her own experiences bringing personal narratives to share in her group (see Chapter 10).
• Through workshopped explorations she brings the visual and aural 'texts' of her body and voice to the process of making theatre (see Body-writing section in Chapter 8).

Director

As with the role of the writer, the role of the director can often be one that comes to dominate group work, not just because a director is likely to be the person in a group with a dominant or forceful personality, but because the group may also be seeking the reassurance of being directed: of being told what to do. Or, sometimes women directors complain that performers turn to them as mother-figures, desiring to be nurtured and looked after (see Kalinska quoted in Caplan 1991: 17). Useful strategies for avoiding this are:

• To share the role of the director between two women at the inception of a project.

- To ensure a director works closely with a dramaturg who is keeping a record of the group's making-process, and relaying ideas between performers and director/s.
- To share the role of director equally among group members.

With the latter strategy you may encounter some of the problems attendant on collective writing. However, if the group has an agreed framework and is certain about its theatrical and feminist directions, then sharing directing can prove a more manageable experience than writing.

If you are working as a mixed majority-of-women group, then you need to think very carefully about whether to have a man in the role of director. Professional women writers have commented on some of the damaging consequences of male directions of their theatre (see Rudet 1986: 180). Sarah Daniels has openly stated her refusal to work with male directors:

> I have, and will always only work with women directors. Yes, I do feel that women writers should help create opportunities for other women working in the theatre and yes, I want my work to say something to other women which is best expressed by another woman BUT more importantly it is about trust – with their track record would you trust a man to direct a feminist play?
>
> (Daniels 1984: 24)

Like Daniels as a writer, many women practitioners feel strongly that it is not possible to have a man in the position of director (see Bassnett 1989: 67). On the other hand, there have been examples of successful writer and director collaboration as, for example, in the partnership between Caryl Churchill as writer and Max Stafford Clark as director. Your group will have to thrash out opinions on this issue should it arise. In the event of your group agreeing to male participation in directing, you may need to argue for some kind of shared model of directing to ensure against the univocal male (mis)direction of women's work. (Note: without prior thought and careful handling it can also be a potentially damaging experience to appoint a bourgeois–feminist woman director to a materialist–feminist company, or to have a middle-class woman directing a working-class women's group, or to have a white woman director directing a Black company, and so on.)

Designer

Given the relatively low levels of funding for professional women's groups, financial constraints conditioned company size (keeping them small), and had an impact on design. Moreover, design for women's companies has been determined by the need to tour. Women's companies have been (mostly) small-scale touring groups, without the resources of a building-based company.

The kinds of project work detailed in this volume assumes, like its professional antecedents, that resources are minimal. My emphasis is on work that takes the form of workshopped presentations rather than large-scale productions. That said, defining and setting your playing or presentation space requires consideration by your group, and may extend into basic stage or lighting designs (depending on the resources at your disposal).

If your work is likely to involve you in design, think about this during the making period; as work that is integral to the making process. Difficulties arise when sets, however basic, are imposed afterwards on the work of the performers. Have discussions about your space, how you want to work in it and any designs for it, early on in your project. Colin Knapp, discussing the role of the designer in devised work in the academy, suggests that a preferred method for the designer is one in which the designer can work with the director before workshopping begins (Knapp 1997: 52). I would modify this suggestion for feminist theatre-making, whether scripted or devised, to suggest that everyone is involved in early discussions (not just the designer and director). If your group is considering and has the resources for a design, ensure that any woman who takes overall responsibility for working in this area is again prepared to work collaboratively: is, at all times, prepared to share and to revise her design with your group.

It may be that a project that is well-resourced financially requires a design team. In this situation try and keep designers and performers working together. Remember, the designers should not have to 'fit in' with the work of the performers. The most successful collaborations are likely to be those arising out of a mutual exchange of inter-dependently generated ideas from the different areas of creative work. A hierarchical division is likely to arise if performers and technicians work in isolation from each other – especially when work is pressured by time and performers are given priority, which tends to be what happens. To help you think about this consider this criticism of the Magdalena 1986 festival:

> Magdalena '86 fell into the bracket of elitist international festivals despite itself. Performers were given precedence over the service women – technicians, designers, crèche workers, etc. – if only through no better motivation than an honest attempt to make up for their lack of comfort and to acknowledge their efforts to come. It remains true though that we did fail to escape from the patrilinear tradition; we were all supposed to do our work and be considered equally creative whether holding a hammer, a light or the stage.
>
> The apparatus didn't change – the performances were in the box, with the technicians hidden from view; there were no curtain calls for them, etc. There was also no discussion about the possible implication of a feminine model. So, many women were excluded from feeling any more affinity with the work than they would have in a mixed group. There was nothing 'new' offered.
>
> (Katy Dymoke, quoted in Bassnett 1989: 73)

To summarise:

• Include designing members of your group at all stages of the work, and at the outset try and ensure that *everyone* has a shared understanding of feminism's, feminist critical theory and proposals for a feminist aesthetic, and so on.
• Avoid a design that is arrived at 'outside' of the group that performers then have to try and work around.
• Ensure that designers and performers collaborate with each other at all stages of the work.
• Do not make designers wait until performers have finished their making. This would mean your work could not benefit from designing ideas, and also that the design aspect is likely to be rushed and marginalised.

This chapter has set out some preliminary thoughts about how you might begin to set up and to organise a group, and to share roles and tasks. Remember these are only guidelines, not rules. There is one important general consideration, however, to which I would recommend you should always give your attention at the outset of a workshop or project and that is to look at the range of skills in your group to help you decide who will be taking responsibility for each area of work. Moreover, always look for ways in which women in your group can share their skills and use them to complement each other. One of the most creative and successful ways I have seen this happen is in the annual 'Performing Words' workshop hosted by the Magdalena Project and lead jointly by Gilly Adams, recognised for her work with professional writers, and Geddy Aniksdal, who is highly trained and skilled in physical theatre. The exchange of skills between these two women provides an instructive and supportive model for the sharing of skills in the group of women participants they are instructing. If in your own groups you have women who see themselves more in the role of dramaturg or writer (as women with more word-based skills), and others as performers (more physically skilled), try to be aware of this, but also to encourage an exchange, so that women are not always drawing on one particular skill, but are also acquiring new ones. Also at the outset be aware of those women who feel they may not have skills to offer, and do not feel secure about the roles or responsibilities they wish to undertake. Try to ensure a supportive and trusting environment, so that all women can find a 'place'. One way to try and achieve this is for all women, no matter what their 'officially' designated task, whether dramaturg, writer, director, performer or designer, to take part in and to experience the exercises your group sets up.

RESOURCES

For further details on the organisation and work of professional feminist theatre companies in Britain see Goodman (1993) and Aston (1997). For details of American companies see Canning (1996). On collaboration and collectives see also Rea (1972), Wandor (1979), Carlson (1988) and Zivanovic (1989).

On the role of the dramaturg see Robson et al. 1990: 54–8. The latter also has useful sections on workshops for writers, detailing some exercises, examples of creative work and listing contact addresses for women's writing workshops in the UK.

Upstaging Big Daddy (Donkin and Clement 1993) offers you several essays that treat the subject of directing women's and feminist work in the USA theatre academy. On the issue of men directing feminist theatre see Lutterbie (*Upstaging Big Daddy*, 1993: 263–276). Donkin (*Upstaging Big Daddy* 1993: 79–87) examines the problems of a white woman directing Black theatre.

On designing for devised theatre in a gender-aware context, see Knapp (1997).

Chapter 3

Finding a body, finding a voice

Any performer who is physically and vocally 'blocked' will be a poor communicator and creator of theatre. Women especially need to free up their bodies and voices from the social and cultural conditioning that has driven them away from themselves, has silenced their voices and has constrained their bodies. Practical suggestions in this chapter, therefore, are designed to put women back in touch with their bodies and their voices. I outline some basic ways that you may find useful to explore and to adapt for relaxing, concentrating, warming up and freeing up the body in preparation for more specialised workshops or performances.

Thinking through the body

> On the one hand, the theatre today puts a demand on the use of the body in a highly active, flexible way. On the other hand, women are pretty much locked into certain senses of their bodies as being too this, too that – the beauty scale is a crucial measuring stick that a woman carries around with her all the time.
>
> (Sklar, quoted in Rea 1974: 85)

I would suggest three basic points to keep in mind when you begin to think about your bodies and as you continue to work:

- body size
- body image
- permission to touch.

Body size

The 'think thin' pressures on women mean that relatively few women feel happy about their bodies or are comfortable with their body weight or size. Feminist psychotherapist Susie Orbach's pioneering *Fat is a Feminist Issue* (1978) highlighted how very few women experience 'self-acceptance' of their bodies. Yet so many of the games or exercises that might be encountered in the theatre workshop impede rather than facilitate women's 'self-acceptance'. To give a concrete example, think about the 'trust circle' exercise. This is widely used in theatre workshops. It involves placing one participant in the centre of a group. She shuts her eyes and 'relaxes', while the group takes her weight and passes her carefully around the circle. In *Playing the Game* Chrissie Poulter emphasises the need for performers to find games that encourage trust and support in the workshop:

> When the work in question is play, it becomes much more important that trust and support exist within the group as many games involve taking a risk, whether physical (blindfold games), social (games which rely on personal information), or creative (improvisation and story-making).
>
> (Poulter 1987: 80)

I agree with the need to trust, but I would also argue that you need to consider the social texts of the physical games that you propose to use. The 'trust circle' is a physical exercise, but women need to think about the social implications of body size in this game. Any woman who feels ill at ease with her size and considers herself to be overweight will hardly feel like relaxing and letting herself go in a trust circle – especially when to begin this exercise a group will often pick the slightest member to experiment with. Heavier women will tend to hold back or opt not to take a turn in the centre of the circle but to keep to a supporting role. As creative work develops they are then more likely to 'fix' themselves in a 'minor' role.

That said, you can work successfully with this (and other weight-bearing) exercises in women-only groups, at a point when self-acceptance is relatively high within the group. My advice to you is always to think to about the social and cultural implications of exercises before deciding to work with them, and to promote trust and support through processes that encourage, rather than discourage, self-acceptance of bodies. (See also advice under the next section, 'Body image'.)

Body image

Allied to body size is body image. For women, looking glamorous tends to equate with feeling good about the body. Being obsessed with 'How do I look?', however, does not help women to be in touch with their bodies. Consider this second quotation from the American feminist director Roberta Sklar:

> In teaching a lot of the physically freeing stuff that developed in the late sixties in experimental theatre, I found it important to focus on where women's minds were as they worked with their bodies. Let me be concrete: a woman often thinks of a certain type of physical movement as callisthenics, as exercise for how her body's going to look. And if that's unshakeable, then it's worthless to do those things with women actresses. If the goal is to free the tension in the body and to develop flexibility, but the head is working on a smaller waistline, it's a useless thing to learn to do the headstand, etc....unless you can break through the callisthenic mind set.
>
> (Sklar quoted in Rea 1974: 85)

In the sections that follow in this chapter are some ideas about physical work that can help to undo this 'mind set' that closes down rather than frees up the body. At the outset you might think about establishing dress codes for your group, which help to put women physically at their ease. Women with a low degree of self-acceptance are going to feel uncomfortable working with Jane-Fonda-look-alikes, so avoid the 'keep-fit' costumes that underpin the 'callisthenic mind set'. Your group might also think about discouraging 'decoration': jewellery (dangerous in workshops because it can easily catch on clothing and cause injury), tight clothing (which restricts breathing, movement, etc.), high-heels (which distort bodies and 'block' voices), and so on. Everyone should be encouraged to wear clothing that offers freedom to move and work, and is a neutral 'canvas' to take on and to take off images. When Zofia Kalinska directed the devised performance *Nominatae Filiae* for the Magdalena Project, she instituted a rule about clothing: 'all performers had to change into clothing in the three basic colours of the performance, red, white and black, and casual clothes were not allowed in the rehearsal room' (Bassnett 1989: 111). Kalinska used this to encourage the ritual aspect of the devised performance work. If your group were starting out with ideas about colour in project work, you could take up Kalinska's colour-coding idea. Or, you might think about staging your own ritual: arriving in outside clothes and changing from these into clothing to work in. Alternatively, you could try having your own 'boutique' workshop in which participants are invited to suggest two or three ideas about clothing. Then the group could decide collectively about what they should wear for work.

Permission to touch

With such a strong emphasis on physical theatre-making, and the foregrounding of the body as a physical 'text' in the 'language' of performance, many workshop activities involve the sculpting of bodies into images.

For example, sculpting techniques broadly based on Boal's forum theatre (group body sculptures are used to image a situation and participants are encouraged to step out and to make changes in order to see what is needed to transform the image/situation), have been widely taken up in workshops as an effective means of creating physical tableaux to initiate social and political change. But in the sculpting exercise, women (and men) need to be clear about the boundaries of touching and need to feel comfortable with being touched, rather than physically invaded, which may give rise to damaging emotional memories. Bernice Fisher advises thinking about ways of respecting women's bodies in sculpting exercises:

> Because women frequently experience violation of their physical boundaries by being touched, activities involving touching cannot be viewed as gender-neutral. Regardless of how safe a given context may seem, women may still bring strong feelings about having their bodies manipulated. For this reason I introduced the sculpting technique by showing participants how they could sculpt each other with respect for each woman's feelings about her body: participants could communicate verbally or non-verbally whether (and how) they wanted to be touched, and the limits of what they were willing to do with their bodies. Such communication fostered sensitivity toward different degrees of physical ability so that, for instance, a mobility-impaired woman could participate in the group sculpture from a seated position.
>
> (Fisher 1994: 193)

'I said body sculpting—not body piercing!':
The DOs and DON'TS of WOMEN in the WORKSHOP

Try to be gender-aware in touching contexts, and always seek permission to touch. Sensitivity towards physical boundaries and respecting how each woman feels about her body being touched will help participants to stay relaxed and focused on the workshopping, rather than feeling anxious and distracted by the possibility of unwanted physical manipulation. Where appropriate, if a woman instructing gives permission and encourages participants to make use of their bodies to communicate or to understand a particular physical exercise, this may also help to put group members at their ease.

Working through the body: warm-up exercises

Any group of performers needs to have a set of warm-up exercises to use regularly at the start of each session to help performers to relax, to concentrate and to energise. For women working together I would suggest that exercises that help them to 'undo' their gender conditioning are particularly useful. You can 'steal' and adapt any number of these from theatre workshops, or relaxation classes. Here are a few suggestions to get you started.

How do I feel?

At the start of each session your group can spend just a few minutes in which members could be invited to share any particular anxieties that they might either have brought with them, or might feel in relation to the work ahead. All women should be encouraged to try and leave worries 'outside' the workshop – and the relaxation exercises that follow are suggested as ways of trying to empty heads/bodies of problems about the family, overdrafts, essay deadlines, mortgages, etc. That said, there may be an immediate upset that a woman cannot quite 'manage' one particular day, and would like the group to be aware of and sensitive to. Similarly, there may be physical injures to alert the group to, for women to be physically caring and careful of one another.

There are two basic premises that are useful for a women's theatre workshop to establish:

*   That a group will aim to be supportive of and sensitive to an individual's emotional and physical well-being.
*   BUT, ultimately, each woman has to take responsibility for her own personal and physical well-being.

Some of the early 1970s work created performances out of emotional memories that simply traumatised and incapacitated participants. For example, Charlotte Rea, describing the work of the American group It's All Right To Be Woman Theatre, stated, that 'performances' were 'often preceded by tears and near-break-down of some of the members because of the difficulty of acting out their personal conflicts and anxieties' (Rea 1972: 82). This is not what I am proposing here. Personal material is a primary re/source for feminist theatre-making, but the distinction between a CR forum and a theatre forum needs to be stressed. A feminist theatre group is not a therapy session.

Partnered and group massage

A gentle massage at the start of a session (or later, in moments of stress and tension) is a pleasurable way to relax the body in preparation for raising concentration and energy levels. Try partnered head, neck and back massages, or your whole group could sit on the floor in a circle with each woman massaging the woman in front of her. Remember that it is important to check how individual women feel about being touched.

Emptying the body

Lie down and make a fist of your left hand and keep this clenched. Starting with your toes and working upwards, tense and relax each body part, breathing deeply all the while. When you have worked all the way up the body, finally let the closed hand open out, slowly. You should feel calm and relaxed at the end of this process.

Follow my body leader[1]

Try walking in your space in a neutral mode. Switch from neutral to a walk where you focus on the part of your body in which you feel most tense. Have a simple game of 'Follow my leader', in which you imitate the leader's tensed body part. Switch back to neutral. Have a good, top-to-toe body shake-out of tension to finish.

Filling the space

> We like to place a lot of emphasis on women taking up space. It's wonderful to see women taking up more space; walking with larger strides on stage, for example, or running with more freedom than they think they are supposed to.
>
> (Ramsden and Winter 1994: 123)

Women are often conditioned into making small, feminine movements and gestures, so your group could try a basic warm-up to encourage them to fill the space. Your group should be encouraged to explore the space and to fill it with large, free movements. When filling the space think about:

• Varying pace and gestures: experiment with speed and physical control.
• Changing directions, avoiding just circling a space and finding creative diagonals and different patterns.
• Changing body levels: not being stuck on one level and experimenting with levels to stretch out into all parts of the body – up high into the fingertips and down low into the knees, etc.
• Stopping and starting: experimenting with physical control. Stops and starts should be clear and controlled.

Circles and sticks: Jill Greenhalgh

This is an excellent training exercise that helps to free up the body, release energy and encourage concentration and co-ordination. Catching and throwing warm-ups are generally useful to women to undo ways in which they may have been socialised into believing themselves to be 'poor' at this kind of activity. The women in your group could first discuss how they feel about their ability to catch and to throw.

In this exercise, women organise themselves into a circle and begin by passing a stick (about a metre long, approximately the size of a broom handle) around the circle, in one direction only, calling out the name of the woman to whom the stick is passed. The stick is thrown from the centre of the body, and needs to be kept as straight as possible for successful throwing and catching. With practice, the number of sticks in the circle can be increased. Drop calling out names (but make sure there is eye contact with a 'catcher' before a stick is thrown), and throw the sticks in any direction around and across the circle. Eventually the group could break the circle altogether and throw the sticks randomly while on the move.

Since Jill Greenhalgh introduced me to this exercise, I have tried it out with both mixed and women-only groups. I have found the mixed-group experience less successful because (some, but not all) men have tended to respond aggressively – throwing with a view to intimidating women participants. Consequently, some women have found it harder to benefit from the exercise; they have retreated into the 'weak'-woman-poor-catcher stereotype. I would suggest, therefore, that women who feel uncertain of their throwing and catching abilities try this warm-up in a women-only context, at least to begin with.

Finding a voice

> Every woman has known the torment of getting up to speak. Her heart racing, at times entirely lost for words, ground and language slipping away — that's how daring a feat, how great a transgression it is for a woman to speak — even just open her mouth — in public. A double distress, for even if she transgresses, her words fall almost always upon the deaf male ear, which hears in language only that which speaks in the masculine.
>
> (Cixous 1981 [1975]: 251)

Women are often afraid of speaking out; of using their voices. Even a vocal, confident woman is often 'acting' confidence. She performs with a confidence that does not allow the voice to come from 'inside' the body. Historically, women have been driven away from their voices, have been socially conditioned into silence, or have been taught that they must speak quietly. We are taught not to shriek or be shrill. We are taught not to express anger. Feminist voice specialists, such as Frankie Armstrong, have highlighted the political implications for women of 'finding a voice':

> We are often systematically robbed of our voices, and a real sense of reunion and recovery can be experienced when we begin to get them back. I believe that the feeling that we have a *right* to be heard is very closely related to our ability to *make* ourselves heard.
>
> For many women, so much anxiety and inhibition has come to surround our voices, particularly when it comes to raising them in volume — really letting rip — that it is truly difficult for us to make ourselves heard in group settings or public meetings.
>
> (Armstrong 1985: 22, original emphasis)

Your group could discuss how they feel about their voices. This can be a very emotional issue. I remember being asked this at the start of a voice workshop with Helen Chadwick. I thought I knew what I was going to say in response, but when it came to my turn to speak, I could hardly say anything for wanting to cry. Somewhere in response to this very simple question lay a hidden history of a quiet child afraid to speak up; a child who had been told repeatedly she was tone deaf and could not sing. Similarly, Frankie Armstrong has commented:

> Somehow, it seems, we learn how *not* to sing. Some natural and spontaneous part of our human inheritance is squeezed and squashed out of us in childhood. The workshops are a safe place in which to recapture some of this birthright, to be given permission to make as loud and liberated sounds as possible, to sing madly out of tune and not be judged for it, to experiment and explore a range of sounds which most of us lose soon after leaving the cot.
>
> (Armstrong 1985: 22, original emphasis)

Therefore, when your group begins to work, try not to place an emphasis on any one woman and encourage equal vocal participation.

An important rule with voice workshopping is always to wear flat shoes or no shoes at all. Heeled shoes introduce physical and vocal distortions, altering posture and movement and 'blocking' the voice.

Massage, relaxation and sound patterns

Always try to include some exercises for relaxation and deep breathing in order to root/route the voice in and through the body, rather than 'lock' the speaking voice in the chest and neck area. Helen Chadwick introduced a partnered massage, concentrating on the head, neck, shoulders and back, ending with one woman, bending over to take the weight of the other on her back, lifting her completely off the floor, in order to open up the spinal area, allowing the body to breathe (see Plate 1). To do this, partners should be of comparable height and weight, so that no woman is self-conscious about her height or body size. Do not attempt lifting if you are someone who has back problems. Relaxing and 'opening' up the voice may be useful as routine, warm-up exercises, and for steadying nerves before a performance.

A single pair of women can take the group through the next stage

Plate 1 Allowing the body to breathe

of workshopping. Find a space for each woman to continue relaxing and breathing, eyes closed and lying flat on the floor. You could use the emptying the body exercise (p. 49) to tense and relax body parts while concentrating on the breathing. Work hard at any body part that you feel is especially 'blocked', tensing and freeing until you feel more relaxed. Remember to keep breathing deeply. Women instructing the group should invite each group member to concentrate solely on her own body and voice and to let out sounds that come from 'inside' her. Further, they should try to help any woman who seems to be 'blocked' by looking for areas of physical tension and gently massaging (with permission). When giving directions, it is important to remember to speak softly to encourage relaxation.

In a second stage of work, women could be invited to focus (with eyes still closed) on other women in the group and (relaxed, breathing deeply) to make whatever sounds they wish as a response to being in the group. Each woman can begin by finding her own sound, but can then allow that to change in response to other sounds she hears within the group.

This vocal patterning can communicate a lot about group dynamics by showing how a group is feeling, or how one woman may be feeling within the group, and so on. This kind of vocal material can be recorded to use in conjunction with other image work.

After relaxation, breathing and vocalising on the floor, always make sure you get up slowly, and in stages. Put your knees together, bend them up, roll on to one side, raise your body into a kneeling position and gradually get back up on to your feet. This helps to avoid feeling dizzy and faint.

Vocal energy

The experience of a group of women singing together can be a powerful and emotional vocal release. In this context I am not thinking about the kinds of singing that most of us feel inhibited by – songs that have to be sung correctly in the right key. Rather, I am thinking about trying to work with songs that come from personal experience – those that have a hidden emotional text. Often, we may not be aware of what this is, or may have forgotten where it comes from, but connecting vocally with material of personal significance helps to free the voice. In the Mothers by Daughters Project detailed in Chapter 10, for example, the women developed a vocal warm-up in which a different woman in each session would teach the group a song from her childhood, connected to her mother. This might be a nursery rhyme, lullaby, or the chorus of a popular tune they recalled their mother singing in the kitchen. Most importantly, the songs came from contexts in which the women had felt safe and secure.

Alternatively, a simple group sound pattern could be attempted. Argentinean director Cristina Castrillo encourages her performers to make sound 'proposals' as part of group work. To give an example:

your group could form a circle and one woman could begin by making a sound that she repeats. Other women in the circle join in one by one until each woman in the group is contributing a sound. When the last woman joins in, the first woman can stop, then the next and so on, until only one voice remains. Any sound making that relates to singing should be discouraged. The need for sounds to come up through the body should be stressed. To encourage vocal energy levels, the group could be encouraged to make the sounds as 'large' as possible. The exercise can be repeated until every woman has had a turn at starting the sound pattern. Again, this vocal 'text' can be recorded to set against image work.

Sounds in words

Do not be afraid to explore the many sound possibilities that words offer. When vocally relaxed and freed up, you can play for as long you like and in many different ways to give your words different lives, different meanings:

• Try out your words in different voices.
• Breathe sounds into your words – your own sounds, sounds from your group.
• Try varying emotions, moods, levels of intensity.

Body and voice check

In suggesting exercises to work on freeing the body and freeing the voice, it might appear as though these are separate. In fact these are very much connected. You need the 'open' body for the voice to speak from 'inside'. As a way of checking on physical and vocal tensions, try paired work in which A 'moves' into a simple line of dialogue coloured by a specific emotion: anger, fear, joy, etc., and B (with permission) physically checks A for any 'blocking' of sounds, or physical tension. If A feels her voice is blocked in a tense shoulder and neck area, B can gently massage the area to release tension.

If participant A has become very tense again – which can often happen when participants concentrate so hard on an instruction, they become vocally and physically incapacitated, then, B can try a 'finger walk' up either side of the spine, starting at the base and 'walking' up through to the neck area. A should be standing, but partly bent over, and should begin to raise the upper part of her body very slowly as B 'walks' her back. This can be repeated two or three times, depending on the degree of physical tension. Participant B can then massage around the neck area of A, using the thumbs to press gently and firmly underneath the shoulder blades and using the palm of the hands to brush down the spine to finish. A can then be asked to repeat her line to see if tension levels have improved. The participants can then swap roles.

Whatever workshop situation, project or production you may be in, exercises such as these are useful both for preparing to work, and for whenever you get physically and creatively 'blocked'. Never be afraid to take a break from production work (especially pre-performance work when tensions are running high), and to take time out for relaxing, 'freeing up' and 'playing'. This can be just the 'break' you need for stimulating creativity.

RESOURCES

On early 1970s women in the workshop see articles by Franey (1973) and Rea (1974). For a more recent discussion of women in the workshop see Ramsden and Winter (1994). See also the accounts of workshopping by American feminist companies in Canning (1996).

Books of games for theatre work, or which you can adapt for theatre work, are very useful sources for 'stealing' ideas from which to develop your own warm-up routines. You might try Barker (1977), Brandes and Phillips (1977), Poulter (1987) or Boal (1992).

On voice, try Armstrong (1975) and (1985), and Cirla (1994). For a theoretical account of an all-female performance experiment with movement and voice see Luckhurst (1996).

Chapter 4

Enter gender

This chapter looks at a series of workshop ideas that focus on introducing gender into the workshop. Suggestions range across gender-themed warm-ups, explorations of the gaze, femininity as masquerade and cross-gendered play. Your group can explore these practical suggestions in different ways: extracting ideas, or collaging together ideas from different themed sessions. Sessions presented here are cross-referenced with other practical ideas and projects detailed in this volume, so dipping in and out of relevant linked sections, rather than any chronological, linear reading may be most useful to you.

You may want to organise a gender workshop as an end in itself: a group of non-theatre students studying gender representation in related disciplines, might, for example, find it useful to 'see' and to experience gender theory in practice. Or, it may be that you select from exercises proposed here as part of 'training' your group in 'disturbing' gender, before moving on to a specific theatre project, whether scripted (see Part II), or devised (see Part III).

Practical suggestions are theoretically premised on the idea that while gender is, as Butler argues, something that we are not free to choose (Butler 1993: x), the 'freedom' of the gender workshop enables us to explore and, potentially, to exploit the gap between the apparatus of gender representation, and ourselves: real, live women, who do not 'fit' the frame designed for us. In alienating gender sign-systems we can play transgressively with our condition as De Lauretis describes it: of being both 'inside and outside the ideology of gender, and conscious of being so, conscious of that twofold pull, of that division, that doubled vision' (de Lauretis 1987: 10). To begin to explore our 'doubled vision', here are some practical suggestions for raising an awareness of how we are looked at.

Introducing the gaze

In Chapter 1 we noted Diamond's proposal that feminist theatre might be able to make an intervention in the gaze. To recapitulate Diamond's point (fundamental to the exercises that follow): 'in my hybrid construction – based in feminist and Brechtian theory – the female performer, unlike her filmic counterpart, connotes not "to-be-looked-at-ness" – the perfect fetish – but rather "looking-at-being-looked-at-ness" or even just "looking-ness" ' (Diamond 1997: 52). While 'looking-ness' might present itself as a possible devising project (see later), you will find it useful to develop warm-ups and short exercises that assist your group in developing an awareness of looking and being looked at.

Eye-to-eye

For workshop sessions with a 'looking-at-to-be-looked-at' focus try warming up with eye-contact games and exercises. For example, try Alison Oddey's concentration circle. Oddey explains as follows:

> Standing in a circle, the person elected to start, A, looks at B and walks slowly across the circle to them. Meanwhile B looks at C, who must say B's name aloud before A reaches B. B is then free to look at D and moves to them, D must look at E, who says D's name before B arrives and D is free to move.
>
> (Oddey 1994: 182)

As Oddey states, this is an excellent concentration exercise. For example, your group can develop it to foreground the emphasis on the task and thematic of looking. Try an additional instruction: when A looks at B and B looks at C, they must all look with lust, anger, passion, desire and so on. You can also experiment with the intensity of the emotion accompanying the look: suggest that a look of lust passes around the circle at level 9 on a scale of 1 to 10, where 10 represents the most intense level. Or try a 'look' of seduction on level 10. Eventually, instructions can cease and group members to can be invited to find their own emotions for looking. Afterwards, the group could discuss the 'looks' to see if they were clear and if they were certain of the emotion (and degree of emotion if you continue to play with intensity levels) attached to the look.

Mirrors

Your group members could sit quietly and concentrate on how they feel about seeing themselves in the mirror. Each participant can be allowed a moment with a mirror to improvise a reaction, a response or an emotion for the rest of the group. After each group member has participated, the group could then discuss mirrors and looking. Each woman might then disclose how she feels about mirrors how and when she uses them.

Talking about mirrors often releases a bundle of contradictions for women: a need to check how we look, in spite of ourselves. Try playing a revisioned game of 'Grandmother's Footsteps' to explore this. In 'Grandmother's Footsteps', participant A stands with her back to the rest of the group who tip-toe towards her. A turns periodically to see if she can catch anyone in the group moving. If she does, they are 'out'. The object of the game is to reach A without being caught.

The game could be modified so that each participant has some sort of pocket mirror. The group have to look as often as they dare into their mirrors without being seen and caught by A. Turning the furtive, guilt-ridden act of 'looking' into a game, helps us towards a healthy laughter at our own self-contradictions.

Try paired mirror work: A is B's mirror and must try to mime each movement of A's, as carefully and as closely as possible. Swap over for B to become A's mirror.

Another game with mirrors is 'Chinese Whispers'. A 'looks' into mirror B, who repeats A's 'look' to mirror C, who repeats this to D, and so on. The last member of the group repeats A's look back to A. It is interesting to note how careful your group has been in passing round the 'look'. How does it mime the original look? How is it distorted?

Your group could try taking improvised mirror responses and turning these into a ritualised sequence of looking and being looked at. Try this by finding a stylised movement for each everyday response, choreographed into a remembered sequence. Sequences can be established individually and eventually choreographed collectively.

Alternatively, switch the focus of your playing from yourselves at the mirror to looking at the object of looking. You might invite every participant to bring a 'looking object' to the session – hand mirrors, cameras, binoculars, magnifying glasses, sunglasses, etc. – and allow space for improvisational, fetishistic play with these objects. Try

finding looking figures or looked-at-figures inspired by the objects
(see Plate 2). The group can then attempt to recognise these figures.

Sadistic narratives of looking

Your group can extend this kind of 'looking' play into developing an
awareness of the ways in which women are often objectified in
narrative organisation. In Mulvey's pioneering work on the gaze and
Hollywood film, she extended the sadistic masculine pleasures of
looking to narrative: 'sadism demands a story, depends on making
something happen, forcing a change in another person, a battle of
will and strength, victory/defeat, all occurring in a linear time with a
beginning and an end' (Mulvey 1992 [1975]: 29). In patriarchal texts
'Woman' is often narratively positioned as 'the one who is done to',
not 'the one who does'. Narratives of women who 'take' the gaze are,
for example, often punished for 'looking' (see Chapter 8 on *The
Bloody Chamber*).

Your dramaturg or group could research narratives of women who
dare to look. Look at a range of different sources – fables, poems,
nursery rhymes, mythology, film, plays. Try acting out the narrative,
and then disturbing the narrative by inserting physical tableaux of
'looking-ness'. Your group can develop these out of work begun in
the 'looking' and 'being-looked-at' improvised mirror sequences.
Hold the tableau to punctuate and to disrupt the linear playing out
of the action. It may help to work with the 'looking-object' props.

Clothes and identity

In an introduction to the photography of Cindy Sherman, feminist
critic Judith Williamson sets out to analyse Sherman's ability to play
with constructions of femininity in the costuming and construction
of herself as 'subject' in some of her early work. In her analysis of
Sherman's 'images of "woman"', Williamson usefully, for our
purposes, touches on the ways in which 'woman', 'femininity' is
constructed through the clothes we wear. Williamson explains:

> When I rummage through my wardrobe in the morning I am
> not merely faced with a choice of what to wear. I am faced with
> a choice of image: the difference between a smart suit and a pair
> of overalls, a leather skirt and a cotton frock, is not just one of
> fabric and style, but one of identity. You know perfectly well that

Plate 2 Medusa in the workshop

you will be seen differently for the whole day, depending on
what you put on; you will appear as a particular kind of woman
with one particular identity *which excludes others*. The black leather
skirt rather rules out girlish innocence, oily overalls tend to
exclude sophistication, ditto smart suit and radical feminism.
Often I have wished I could put them all on together, or appear
simultaneously in every possible outfit, just to say, Fuck you for
thinking any one of these is *me*. But also, See, I can be all of them.
(Williamson 1983: 102)

Your group could begin by discussing their different dress codes and
how this changes their self-representation. Group members could be
encouraged to bring in clothing from their own wardrobes, to
improvise with the clothing for the rest of the group and to caption
how they see themselves. Focus on how a different outfit/identity
makes a woman feel: more or less vulnerable, empowered or disempowered and so on.

Experiment with mixing your clothes/identities in an exploration
of Judith Williamson's angry 'Fuck you for thinking any one of these
is *me*' (see also Chapter 10, p. 189). Your group might want to try this
in the form of an improvised monologue, putting on different
layers/identities and seeing how this changes your 'selves'. This kind
of exploration may have implications for how you 'see' yourselves
and how you feel you are seen by others, both in the space of the
workshop, and out on the streets.

Invite someone else in your group to put on one of your 'identities', while you narrate your identity. Try narrating identity in both
the first and the third person. Put on another of your own items of
clothing and invite another woman in your group to narrate your
identity, also switching between different modes of first- and third-
person narration. In the gaps between bodies, clothes and narrations
what changes? What feels different? What do you see differently?

While we may, as Butler objects, always be in the position of
choosing from images (gender identities) that are decided for us (Butler
1993: x), in the workshop, on stage or, even in the re-presentation of
our own dress codes, we begin to alienate an identity we have 'chosen'.

Femininity as masquerade

Looking at how we look and are looked at makes us aware of the
need to signal 'but that's not me'. We have already noted the impossi-

bility of 'freeing' ourselves from the gender sign-system, but, we can begin to glimpse the necessity and desirability of its re-production as a 'spectacle' of refusal.

In this section, I suggest themed sessions that focus on ways of exploring what happens when the feminist performer disturbs the sign of the feminine, or rather, *how* she can demonstrate femininity in order to refuse it. In particular, I wish to introduce the concept of femininity as masquerade, and practical ways of masquerading.

Masquerade in theory

The idea of femininity as masquerade comes from a feminist reading of the Lacanian model of representation and subjectivity, in which the feminine constitutes a masquerade because it is 'other' than the male sign and discourse, and can only be its copy. However, what happens if a woman decides to copy the copy? Theoretically, Luce Irigaray proposes this as one way in which woman might begin to 'undo' the constraints of patriarchy:

> Here is a theatrical staging of the mime: miming the miming imposed on woman, Irigaray's subtle specular move (her mimicry *mirrors* that of all women) intends to *undo* the effects of phallocentric discourse simply by *overdoing* them....Irigaray's undermining of patriarchy through the overmiming of its discourses may be the one way out of the straitjacket of phallocentrism.
>
> (Moi 1985: 140)

The concept of '*overdoing*' Woman, of 'miming the miming imposed on woman', has been taken up in film (see Doane on masquerade 1992 [1982]) and theatre (see Diamond 1989b). Diamond cites some practical examples, which include Lois Weaver's Tammy Whynot, where Weaver 'mimics the carefully choreographed gestures and bittersweet seductiveness of a country music star', and Italian performer and writer Franca Rame's use of 'dyed blond hair and heavy makeup to mimic the gender signs of heterosexual femininity' (Diamond 1989b: 66). (See also Chapter 6 on 'Mimicry', p. 119.)

You may also find some of Cindy Sherman's early photography useful to you to help with the conceptualisation of the 'overplaying' femininity strategy. Have a look at some of Sherman's photographs in which she is author and subject of images that overplay the representational system of Woman, making visible the 'naturalised' codes of femininity. Have a look, for example, at Sherman's series of untitled black-and-white photographs in which she de-familiarises familiar cinematic representations of woman (see Williamson 1983).

Discussion of Sherman's photography will also alert you to feminist debate on the efficacy of masquerade as a strategy for disturbing the sign of the feminine. While we can never 'police' the reception of images, if we fail to clearly signal the register and discourse of 'overdoing', we shall merely be presenting the Lacanian model, not 'undoing' it. Over-glamorous images may simply be read as glamorous. This happened when Monstrous Regiment tried to critique glamour in their late 1970s production of Bryony Lavery's *Time Gentlemen Please* (Hanna 1991: xlii–iii), and when 1980s British cabaret group Fascinating Aïda tried to work in producing overglamorised versions of the white middle-class, materially 'successful' woman of the 1980s, which tended to slip into a celebration of glamour rather than critique. In brief, to 'overdo' femininity we need to try and re-present it in quotation marks: to make it clear to the spectator that our aim is to 'undo' not to affirm.

The vocabulary of the feminine

If we want to try 'overplaying' femininity, then we need to heighten our awareness of how the sign of the feminine is constructed. Nineteenth-century actors had handbooks that instructed them on poses for the externalisation of emotions in which masculinity and femininity were clearly marked. Illustrations from these are useful for re-presentational play (see the Resources section). Such images may already seem 'overdone' to us in their histrionic 'staginess', which is alien to our twentieth-century conventions of realism, although this makes them useful for disturbing realism. Your group could try a scene from a realist play in which you punctuate moments of playing with histrionic poses of femininity (and masculinity) that break up the action (for more on this point, see Chapter 6).

For a twentieth-century 'handbook' on gender sign-systems you might try using advertisements. Organise your group to find a range of advertisements that represent 'Woman'. Look at the way in which 'She' is constructed. Look at the vocabulary of her body 'parts', how they are put together, how they 'speak' meaning, and so on. Erving Goffman's *Gender Advertisements* (1987 [1976]) is a good reference point for this. Goffman sets out series of advertising images to show how gender is encoded in commercial representations of the family, or how women are codified as the feminine in the business of selling. Try working on a particular body part to explore how it 'speaks' the feminine. Take the hand for example, and, using the advertisements to guide you, see if you can find a vocabulary for a series of feminine hand gestures. Show these to the group. See if they can 'name' them. (One of the ways in which you can increase your awareness of femininity encoded in hand gestures is to paint your nails. This has the effect of alienating hands from the rest of your body.)

Try this in reverse. The group could come up with a series of proposals that they would like to see expressed through feminine hand gestures. For example, how are statements such as 'I am beautiful', or 'I am angry' spoken through hands in the vocabulary of the feminine. Your group could work on the vocabulary of the feminine in different body parts.

'In your face'

Women's magazines are an excellent resource for highlighting the gap between the fictions of femininity and the 'real'; between 'Woman' and ourselves as 'misfit' women.

You might start with a pile of different women's magazines collected by the group. Try taking the covers off these to make a large collage. Survey your wall of smiling cover girl faces and play against these with your own faces: slip into grotesque smiles and eye movements. Feel what happens to your face as you put on and take off the cover-girl smile.

Try staging a gallery of poses based on images inside the magazine. Again, you might wish to collage these to work from. Try re-presenting the poses by making them as large as you can. See what happens if you alter the facial expressions that accompany them. Experiment between a neutral stance and an over-the-top model pose. Organise your own cat-walk of re-presented poses.

Your group could work on a short story in a women's magazine. Use a Brechtian style of reported narration to distance yourselves from the story. Use freeze-frames to bring about pauses in the action and to interrogate gender roles in the narrative. Use pauses as interruptions in which a group member can direct a change in events. Try playing out alternative endings.

You can carry on through magazines in this way. Problem pages that tend to be so divorced from the difficulties that women face in their real lives can make satirical, if not surreal, oppositional sequences. You may even decide to develop a project out of this material that takes the magazine as its format. Gay Sweatshop, for example, in their 1994 production *In Your Face* presented their exploration of gay sexualities against a backdrop of *Vogue* covers, contents and images. Stepping in and out of the *Vogue* pages (projected into the playing space), performers queered the heterosexual images through the on-stage exploration of their marginalised sexualities.

Icons

Pop stars or film stars may promote certain 'styles' of femininity or masculinity. We are all surrounded by and often influenced (despite ourselves) by the glamour of film, television and music — especially during adolescence. Find out who your female pop or film icons were or are. Your group could bring in photographs, tapes and videos to demonstrate the representations of femininity. Look at gestural encodings in music and cinematic performances. Remember: what you are researching is not the figure 'herself', but her representation, and your aim is to re-present the representation. You are not trying to 'be' the star, you are miming the mime of the star. So use exaggerated gestures. Try a badly synchronised miming to the songs of a pop star, or miming the gestures and words of a movie star against a video recording in the style of a badly dubbed film, and so on.

The boutique

(Your group may want to organise a two-part workshop: part one in which you work with your own clothes on a dress and identity session, as described earlier, and part two in which you explore costuming and gender stereotypes. You should expect an emotional contrast between working on your own self-representation and the exploration of stereotypes, as proposed in the following two workshop suggestions.)

Your group could choose up to three items of conventional, feminine clothing from your theatrical costume store. If you do not have access to such a store, then your group could visit a charity shop or jumble sale where you can purchase items of clothing cheaply.

Bring your selections back to your space and arrange a display of them. You can do this in different ways. Try pegging the items of clothing up on studio drapes so that the space is transformed into a 'boutique' of assorted costuming. Where this is not possible, chairs, tables, rostra, scaffolding, or any available surfaces in the working space can be used for creating a boutique-styled display. This way, the clothing begins to transform into oddly 'deformed' body shapes. Getting outfits pegged up on coat hangers is an excellent way of heightening the sense of deformation. Make your space as full as possible.

Group members can then 'stroll' through the 'boutique' and have a good look around. Each participant then chooses one item to begin to work with and focuses on the gender stereotype suggested by the clothing. Explore the gestures, movements and facial expression that accompany the stereotype. Improvise and explore these until you can put them 'on' and take them 'off'. Switch between neutral and stereotype. Play with the putting on of the stereotype until this is as exaggerated as you can make it. You should aim for a cartoon style.

Try creating a cartoon narrative for the 'overplayed' stereotype. You might start with the whole group focusing on a single stereotype, suggesting a narrative and playing this out in a sequence of freeze-framed cartoon-type tableaux. This could become more complicated by allowing a cartoon narrative to develop by putting more than one 'overplayed' stereotype together and seeing what happens.

'Fashioning' the body

Women have always been victims of fashion. Our bodies are always supposed to be a 'perfect', 'feminine' 'fit'. Body parts have to be fashioned, that is to say squeezed, reduced or enlarged into a 'feminine ideal'. Organising a themed workshop on fashion and the body can help to expose the ideological pressures of the 'feminine Woman' on women.

Your dramaturg or group could research materials on histories of fashion and the body. A collage could be set up to be looked at and shared with the group. A particular body part could be selected to work on and a group sculpture made that foregrounds the body part. Each woman should be allowed to move into the body-part image and to modify the sculpture until there is a group consensus. Each woman could be invited to caption the body part with a brief description – fix artificial smiles, and so on.

Think about physical exercises that you can use to represent the pain that fashion causes. For example, a student project on the theme of 'undressing the past' tried to find ways of imaging how various (man–made) designs in nineteenth-century corsetry might have affected the body. We tried raised human wheelbarrows – where the supporting partner raises the 'barrow' off the ground – as a way of imaging the pain and violence inflicted on the body by the corset. If you want to try this, work slowly at first, with A holding B at the waist. B clasps legs behind A's middle who acts as a support and lever to raise B off the ground (see Plate 3). With practice you can repeat this action and speed it up.

You can 'fashion' a whole project by looking at different body parts and looking historically at how specific cultures have shaped these. The monstrous ways in which women's bodies have been forced into different shapes lends itself to an 'overplaying' style of exaggerated, grotesque comedy, which, combined with a high degree of (safe) physical exertion in performance, makes visible the pain inflicted on the body through ideologies of femininity.

You might try exploring this in physical circus-style routines. You can keep these very simple. For example, try bits of juggling, forward rolls, supported wheelbarrows or cartwheels. Always make sure your group has mats for working on. Remember that you should not over-exert yourselves as performers to the point where you endanger your bodies. Your aim is not to be in pain, but to work in a physical performance register that demonstrates the pain of fashion on the body.

If you introduce a ring'master' into your 'circus', you can also try using this figure to create a Brechtian-styled narration of body parts. As a point of reference for thinking about this kind of project work, try Bobby Baker's show *Take a Peek!* (see the Resources section), which turns the spectacle of a woman's body into a grotesque circus or fairground-styled peep show.

'Hysterics' in the workshop

In Irigaray's psychoanalytical framing of patriarchy we noted that 'Woman' cannot be heard to speak unless she mimes herself in the discourse of the masculine, a condition that Irigaray describes as a form of hysteria (see Moi 1985: 135). In our practice, can the figure of the hysteric offer us ways of 'seeing' the mimetic/hysteric feminine condition of the psychoanalytical frame? A question that feminist critic Elaine Showalter asks is whether hysteria can be read as a form of 'feminist protest' on the part of women who had no other means of fighting back (Showalter 1987 [1985]: 147)? If we

Plate 3 'Wheelbarrows'

perform the hysteric, who is herself a performer, who corporeally represents her 'condition' to an audience of male doctors, can we
re-present the hysteric/hysteria as feminist protester/protest against
the sign of the feminine?

The attraction of the hysteric as a figure to give practical exploration to the dangers and dangerous excesses of femininity was

brought to my attention through learning about the research, work-shopping and production of Anna Furse's *Augustine*, performed by Paines Plough in 1991. Furse researched the figure of the late nine-teenth-century hysteric, Augustine, who was a patient of Jean-Martin Charcot's at the Salpêtrière clinic in Paris. Charcot specialised in the treatment of hysteria, particularly female hysteria, and some of his women patients, like Augustine, became celebrities, were endlessly photographed and 'performed' their hysteria at Charcot's public lectures. Augstine's real-life narrative is a narrative of child abuse. Her hysterical symptoms began at the age of 13 after she had been raped at knife-point by her employer, who was also her mother's lover (Furse 1997: 3).

In workshopping her Augustine research materials, Furse used exercises that focused on 'writing' signs on the body. To give an example: try a paired exchange in which each woman tells her partner an emotional narrative. The partner must tell the story back to the narrator without words but using gestures and sounds. Repeat this reducing the visual narrative pattern to a gestural core: a single gesture and sound that is the 'key' to the narrative. Try this again as a hand or foot narrative, again reducing these to an emotional narrative core.

Try setting up physical tableaux that re-present a day-in-the-life of 'the wife at home', or, 'the mother with young children'. Base this on reproducing the representations of these figures (rather than the reality of lives). When you have explored these extensively, and have a day-in the-life series, where possible try and photograph these, just as Charcot photographed his patients. Make your poses as clear and larger-than-life (rather than real life) as you can.

You can go on to work with the photographs you have taken. Study these and put captions to them. When Charcot photographed Augustine in the *attitudes passionelles*, the third phase of the three-phase seizure known as *grand hystérie*, Charcot gave these 'subtitles' such as ' "amorous supplication", "ecstasy", "eroticism" ' (Showalter 1987 [1985]: 150).[1] So a wife-at-home series might have poses that are captioned 'devotion', 'duty', 'domestication'. Re-present your poses against projections of the photographs.

Your group could try turning the still, larger-than-life, subtitled poses into a cartoon-styled, clowning routine (see earlier under 'Fashioning' the body'). Set up your poses again and try telling the 'real' story 'behind' the image. Try Furse's hand narratives to tell the 'real' story. Explore the 'gap' between the representation and the 'real'.

Your group might go on to work in similar ways, but instead of setting up a modern day-in-the-life-of series, try working on 'classic' female 'hysterics'. These might include case histories such as Augustine or Dora (see next section), but you might also try working with fictional representations such as Shakespeare's Ophelia in *Hamlet*. Look, for example, at the cultural production of Ophelia as 'hysteric', in art or literature. Explore 'hysterical' poses for Ophelia and overmime these. Try clowning in a circus-style register, and so on. Embodied in Augustine's *attitudes passionelles* was her narrative of abuse and rape. What would Ophelia's narrative be? Can she be heard or re-figured differently?

Re-figuring the 'Woman'/hysteric in the narrative

> When Luce Irigaray rewrites Freud's essay on 'Femininity', inscribing her own critical voice into his tightly woven argumentation and creating an effect of distance, like a discordant echo, which ruptures the coherence of address and dislocates meaning, she is performing, enacting, the division of women in discourse. When others after her – writers, critics, filmmakers – turn back the question on itself and remake the story of Dora, *Boheme*, Rebecca or Oedipus, opening up a space of contradiction in which to demonstrate the non-coincidence of woman and women, they also destabilise and finally alter the meaning of those representations.
>
> (de Lauretis 1984: 7)

As de Lauretis suggests, 'remaking' or re-telling stories represents fertile ground for the feminist practitioner (see Chapters 8 and 9). Using a combination of feminist critical theory, and physical story-telling to redirect a patriarchal scene is one way of re-figuring the Woman in the narrative. This technique surfaces in many of the working examples in this study. Here, I should like to give you some brief notes on working with feminist theory, and sound and body texts, to re-figure the hysteric/'Woman' as a final, synthesis example in the section on masquerade.

This practical example comes from a workshop devoted to re-figuring Freud through Cixous. The source texts for this are Freud's case study of Dora (Freud 1977), Cixous's essay 'Aller à la mer'

(1984), and Cixous/Benmussa's re-telling of the Dora story (see Chapter 1, pp. 10–11).[2]

The re-presentation of Dora by Cixous and Benmussa is a way of disrupting the 'master' narrative. It works semiotically through dreams, images, screens, sounds, etc. to challenge the power relations of doctor and patient in order for the spectator to 'see' a different narrative. In re-figuring the 'father', the voice of Dora begins to be heard.

Following the voice instructions given on p. 52, your group should relax, breathe deeply and focus on the image of Cixous's Dora. While concentrating on this image, group members should release sounds. Make a tape of these sounds.

Your group could then project an image of Freud and participants could be asked to focus instead on the Dora in Freud's case study: the Dora who is coughing, hoarse, and unable to speak. One by one, group members could be added 'into' the projection and invited to 'mime' the sounds they associate with Dora, Freud's 'hysterical' patient. They could be encouraged to respond emotionally, opening their mouths wide, but without releasing sounds (see Plate 4). This could be played with a few times to fully explore responses. Group members could be encouraged to add in gestures to their silent sound-making.

Re-play the 'hysterical' Dora against the sound tape of Cixous's Dora. Try giving your group Cixous's plea for women to tell a different story. (If possible, it helps to project this in your playing space):

> No need for plot or action; a single gesture is enough, but one that can transform the world. Take for example this movement of women towards life, passed on from one woman to another, this outstretched hand which touches and transmits meaning, a single gesture unfolding throughout the ages, and it is a different Story.
>
> (Cixous 1984: 547)

Each group member could be invited to find physical responses, reduced to a single individual gesture. Furse's hand narratives could be used to work on this. The responses could be organised into a group tableau. Experiment with the gestures of a 'different Story' and the sound tape.

When we start to 'remake' the stories, then we begin to see them differently: 'You only have to look at the Medusa straight on to see

Plate 4 Re-figuring the Father

her. And she's not deadly. She's beautiful and she's laughing' (Cixous 1981 [1975]: 255).

Crossing gender sign-systems

While the figure of the hysteric offers the dangerous possibility of disturbing the sign of the feminine imposed on women, the danger to the hysteric (and by implication to women) must not be overlooked. Over time, Augustine's hysterical 'star' turns resulted in increasingly violent behaviour. A risk to herself and to others, she was confined to a cell, but managed to escape from the clinic by disguising herself as a man. Furse represented this moment of 'escape' theatrically by bringing on Augustine dressed as a male impersonator of nineteenth-century music hall.

Cross-dressing, cross-gendering techniques represent a theatrically exciting way of demonstrating and de-automatising our perception of 'naturalised' gender sign-systems (see also cross-gender playing in Chapter 5). Crossing the gender divide may expose the way in which gender is organised as an arbitrary, artificial sign-system, which, like all such systems, it is possible to disturb and to deconstruct.

Theatrical traditions of impersonation are extensive and well-documented (see the Resources section). Your dramaturg or group could research specific aspects of impersonation and note the details of different male and female cross-dressing traditions in different cultures. For example, Maya Chowdray's *Kaahini* (1997) for Red Ladder Theatre, examined gender through Asian cultures, researching shamanic rituals in which men and women exchange genders. (Chowdhry used a story from *The Mahabharata*, in which, after a dream where Shiva tells a king his wife will bear him a son, the king raises his daughter as a son.)

If you are working in a mixed group you might want to discuss reactions to cross-gendered play. It is generally the case that women readily accept playing male roles as a convention of the workshop, whereas men often react negatively (hysterically) to the idea of playing women's roles. Asking men to play women seriously (rather than comically, as in the tradition of the pantomime dame), is an issue, therefore, which you may need to discuss and negotiate in a mixed group.

Masculine and feminine vocabularies

Go back to your collage of advertisements and where necessary add in further advertising images that help to underscore the construction of both femininity and masculinity. You might like to try Griselda Pollock's idea of gender reversal (1992 [1977]: 136–7), and produce a collage of advertisements where you reverse visual and textual references to gender. In the workshop you can use this as a guide to help you 'stage' your own corporeal masculine and feminine vocabularies.

Begin with a simple action, possibly one imaged in your collage, and try playing this action in 'neutral', 'masculine' and 'feminine' modes. You might start, for example, with sitting in a chair, and then develop this into a sequence of sitting, getting up, and walking in each of the three modes, until you are able to switch confidently between each of these. Explore and exchange different sets of actions in your group.

When group members have experienced crossing between masculine and feminine sets of actions, the work could move on by crossing a 'masculine' walk with a woman's role. You could use either a scripted scene or a constructed scene of your own for this. See what happens when you act out a scene and change the gender of pronouns so, for example, a character that everyone can see is a 'she' is referred to as a 'he'.

Your group members could bring in their most masculine item of clothing and their most feminine item of clothing to a workshop. Organise a series of actions that are explored in a neutral mode, and are then repeated using the masculine and feminine clothing props. See what happens to bodies and to voices when you switch between these different registers. Try a scripted scene in which your performers cross-dress and play across gender. You do not have to do this fully costumed. You can use minimal masculine and feminine vestimentary props for this exploration.

Research gender myths from other cultures to play against our Western insistence on a 'true sex'. Or, examine our Western insistence on the male/female divide by playing out roles in which characters are not 'fixed' in their opposite sex, but constantly play between the two, referring to themselves as she and he.

Research the lives of women who cross-dressed as men (see Resources) to understand the social, cultural and economic constraints that encouraged them into life-long cross-gendered masquerades. Using your research, construct short gestic scenes that demonstrate the need to 'pass' as a man.

Go back to the narratives of women who dared to look, and play these out again reversing gender roles. If, for example, you work on Tennyson's poem, *The Lady of Shallot* (a 'classic' narrative of 'Woman' punished for looking), what happens if you imprison Lancelot in the tower, and have the Lady of Shallot riding by on horseback? As a variant on this, what happens where both Lancelot and the Lady are female and the gaze passes between women?

Try thinking of celebrated female figures constrained by the material production of femininity in their particular historical moment and play out a fantasy of what your figure might have liked to do, if she had been a man. What would it have meant for Queen Elizabeth 1 to have been 'King Elizabeth 1'?

Using the way in which Furse stages Augustine's exit from the patriarchal scene as your working example, find 'doomed' stage heroines to work on, and allow them a fantasy exit, dressed as a man. What happens, for example, if, instead of shooting herself, Ibsen's Hedda Gabler escapes her 'fate' in male guise?

Think about your own lives: are there moments when gender restricted your choice? Invite your group to act out or image these restrictions and then to play out cross-gendered alternatives.

Finally, try working from the voice warm-up described on p. 52. Your group can then move on to make their most masculine and most feminine sounds. It is important to stress that participants should not try and intellectualise what this means, but should 'body-think' their responses. Try taping these. Your group can then develop sets of masculine and feminine gestures and experiment with crossing feminine sounds with masculine gestures and vice versa. You might also like to try another recording that mixes both sets of sounds and to experiment with this against mixing gendered gestures in the body. Use your tapes with other practical suggestions listed above.

These three chapters in Part I – on the organisation of woman-centred and feminist theatre work, on the preparation of bodies and voices for workshopping and on theory–practice explorations of gender representation – are ones you can re-visit whether you opt to work in a scripted (see Part II) or non-scripted (see Part III) theatre context. In brief, remember that:

- a feminist text is unlikely to be successful (i.e. politically, creatively and aesthetically effective) if you end up working and performing in an hierarchical, masculinist context;
- whatever the workshop or performance situation you are in, you need to be in touch with bodies and voices. This may mean paying regular attention to 'undoing' the social and cultural constraints that 'block' the freedom to move, the freedom to speak;
- including gender-themed workshops as an integral part of scripted or devised theatre projects is an effective way to 'train' your group in the many techniques and methods of disturbing gender.

RESOURCES

For a nineteenth-century stage handbook try *Practical Illustrations of Rhetorical Gesture and Action, adapted to the English Drama* (London: Richard Phillips, 1807) by Henry Seddons. This has excellent figures marked up as 'Affection', 'Despair', or 'Love', etc. These can help with practical explorations of gender, class and status. For illustrative material you can also try the Pictorial Archival series, which has a volume on *Women: A Pictorial Archive from Nineteenth-Century Sources*, compiled by Jim Harter (revised edition, New York: Dover, 1982 [1978]). I also came across an illustrated article 'The Art of Gesture' in the *Strand Magazine*, December 1910, which has a wonderful series of captioned images contrasting the gestures of English and continental women.

If you are looking for modern advertising sources then try Goffman (1987 [1976]). Janice Winship's *Inside Women's Magazines* (London: Pandora, 1987) also has useful illustrative material and textual extracts from a range of historical and contemporary magazines which might prove helpful to you.

Jo Spence's notes for a television programme on women's breasts, see 'Tip of the Iceberg' (Spence 1995: 124–8), are a useful point of reference for thinking about work on female body parts (see in particular her section on visual imagery, pp. 126–8). For a performance example of re-presenting the female body through a style of clowning see Bobby Baker's video *Take a Peek!: London International Festival of Theatre* (1995) in her 'Daily Life' series, distributed by Artsadmin, London.

For visual material on female hysterics try the illustrations in Furse (1997) (Furse also lists the archival sources from which she worked). Also useful are photographs of some of the star nineteenth-century actresses who worked in the histrionic style. Photographs of Sarah Bernhardt, for example, (an actress who made a point of going to see Augustine's 'performances'), would be helpful to you in this context. If you are looking for stories about female 'hysterics' to adapt (see Chapter 8) then you might try Alison Fell (ed.) *Serious Hysterics* (London: Serpent's Tail, 1992).

For an essay detailing production work on Cixous/Benmussa's *Dora* see Forte and Sumption (1993). For further thoughts on working with feminist theory in performance see Austin (1993).

For a study of the lives of women who cross-dressed as men, see Julie Wheelwright's *Amazons and Military Maids* (London: Pandora,1989). On cross-dressing in the theatre try Marjorie Garber's *Vested Interests* (London and New York: Routledge, 1992), or Leslie Ferris (ed.) *Crossing the Stage* (London and New York: Routledge, 1993). For plays on the subject of cross-dressing try Simone Benmussa's *The Singular Life of Albert Nobbs* (in Benmussa 1979); Erika Block's *Walking On Peas* in *Contemporary Theatre Review*, vol. 6, no. 3, 1997, and Caryl Churchill's *Cloud Nine* in *Plays One* (London: Methuen, 1985).

For workshopping on gender and gesture see Zeig (1985). On 'Drag King' workshops see Solomon (1997) 'Epilogue: Not just a passing fancy: notes on butch'.

Part II

Dramatic texts, feminist contexts

Part II offers three chapters that are all concerned with working from dramatic scripts in feminist contexts. Chapter 5 examines feminist ways to work on canonical texts, Chapter 6 looks specifically at working with woman-authored realism, and Chapter 7 addresses the question of how to find performance registers for feminist scripts.

It may seem odd in a volume such as this to look at plays that have acquired canonical status, or drama that is working through a dominant dramatic form, even if authored by women. However, if we do not examine mainstream theatre or the politics of a conventional theatrical form, we leave them unchallenged. I've paid particular attention in Part II to form and structure. This is not because I am advocating a structuralist position, rather, that if we can understand a structure, understand how a text is made and put together, we are equipped to 'unmake' it, to pull it apart and to begin to make it our own. This is something that the feminist performer may find she needs to do to resist the cultural authority of 'master' texts; to play in the realist gaps from the past, and even to find a feminist aesthetic, style and register to activate the feminist script.

Chapter 5

'Cultural sniping'

Since the 1970s feminist literary studies have established a body of scholarship concerned with challenging the value systems that govern and determine the literary canon. Such studies have revealed how the canon is based on those value systems that also dominate our systems of (capitalist) economic and (patriarchal) social control, and have, in consequence, highlighted its gender bias. Feminist approaches to the canon have worked both to read canonical 'master' texts from a feminist perspective, taking account of gender, race and class, and to discover 'lost' work by women writers, which the value systems of the canon have obscured from view. This latter direction is pursued in the following chapter. Here, I am concerned with how, as women/feminist theatre-makers, we can challenge canonical 'master-pieces' through a feminist theatre practice.

Why make a feminist intervention?

First, you need to consider why it is necessary to engage in such a practice, rather than, for example, opting to work exclusively in the canonical margins, where much of women's work is culturally located.

At The Glass Ceiling Conference in 1991 hosted by the Women's Theatre Group (subsequently re-named the Sphinx), feminist scholar Janet Todd's plenary on the playwright Aphra Behn raised a number of canonical issues. If it were possible to trace how and why Behn came to be marginalised in the history of the stage, then why, Todd was asked, was it still the case that Behn was not, subsequent to her feminist recovery, becoming more visible. Todd's response focused on the canon:

I'm sure it has much more to do with the canonisation of major
male figures than it has to do with anything else. After all, there's
200 years of it, it's not just now....Why Behn is not making it
now, I don't know. She's not being taught much in Universities
yet, which is part of the problem....My colleagues might think
it's ludicrous to have a course on Aphra Behn, while they would
be quite happy to have a course on Charles Dickens, or
Congreve.

(Todd n.d.: 31)

Todd's comments draw attention to the ways in which feminist
scholarship is struggling against a two-hundred-year tradition of 'the
canonisation of major male figures'. In the face of such a long-
standing and male-biased tradition, it is hard, as Todd notes in the
Behn example, to effect a radical shift away from the 'masters'. This
accounts for why the study of women's drama and theatre takes place
mostly in specially designed courses offered alongside the canonical,
or, through the addition of one or two women writers to the canonical syllabus. It also reinforces the need for feminist resistance to
rather than acceptance of the canonical in the interests of, for
example, seeing 'an abundance of Aphra Behn', rather than 'an over-
abundance of Shakespeare' (plenary discussion, Todd n.d.: 31). Or, as
feminist Renaissance scholar Kathleen McLuskie writes, 'feminist
criticism must...assert the power of resistance, subverting rather than
co-opting the domination of the patriarchal Bard' (McLuskie 1985:
106).

Resisting performers and cultural snipers

However, if we cannot effect an immediate, radical shift in the canon,
we can attend to the ways in which we approach and study it. There
are two concepts that I feel may be useful to you to begin to frame a
feminist workshopping of the canonical: the resisting performer and
the cultural sniper.

The resisting performer is a proposal derived from Judith Fetterly's
concept of the 'resisting reader' (Fetterly 1978): the feminist reader
who has to resist the ideological work of the 'master' text. Fetterly
was working on American fiction, but you can adapt her idea for a
theatre context. Jill Dolan, for example, applies Fetterly's concept of
the 'resisting reader' to the feminist theatre critic 'who analyses a
performance's meaning by reading against the grain of stereotypes

and resisting the manipulation of both the performance text and the cultural text that it helps to shape' (Dolan 1988: 2). You might extend this further to describe the role of the performer. Your task will be to take on the role of resisting agent or performer who functions as an ideological, cultural and theatrical demonstrator – empowered as the feminist critic (rather than female victim) of the 'master' text.

Cultural sniping is a concept proposed by the photographer Jo Spence (1995). Spence's photograph of herself as 'Cultural Sniper' (1995: 162) depicts her naked, with daubed-on (warlike) paint, and a terrorist-styled black stocking over her head to mask her identity. The aggressive set of Spence's eyes and mouth combine with the image of her armed with a catapult, which she is about to fire (at the spectator). This is the 'little' woman (David) attacking, 'sniping' at the dominant systems of social and cultural representations (Goliath), and challenging the gaze of her viewer.

Spence composed the photograph as a response to an identity crisis: in masquerading, or 'passing' in middle-class culture, she felt she had lost touch with herself and her working-class roots. She captioned the image with the following explanation:

> A crisis of identity culminating in my trying to tell myself a story of who I thought I was. I finally came up with an image which had evaded me, one which was structurally absent from my previous photographic discourse, the image of myself as 'Cultural Sniper', capable of appearing anywhere, in any guise.
>
> (Spence 1995: 162)

You can think about Spence's cultural identity crisis in relation to how you feel about our dominant culture, but also use her cultural sniping tactic to fight back. As a cultural terrorist, like Spence in her photograph, you might not be able to win the war against Shakespeare, or other 'icononicals', but you can offer pockets of resistance.

In the practical suggestions for theatrical cultural sniping that follow, I have used Shakespeare's *King Lear* as an 'icononical' point of reference. The re-production of Lear as the play's emotional centre, and the attendant demonisation of the two older daughters and the idolisation of the youngest, make it especially difficult, but, in consequence all the more necessary, to resist. As Kathleen McLuskie argues, no 'purpose [is] served by merely denouncing the text's misogyny, for *King Lear's* position at the centre of the Shakespeare

the 'masters' in pieces:
CULTURAL SNIPING as FEMINIST PRACTICE

canon is assured by its continual reproduction in education and the theatre and is unlikely to be shifted by feminist sabre-rattling' (McLuskie 1985: 102). (An aside: your group may wish to ponder this point further, and perhaps have a look across at one or two of

Shakespeare's comedies, reputedly, as Penny Gay argues (1994: 3), more transgressive in terms of gender representation.)

Shakespeare the 'icononical'

Writing this chapter proved to be the most troublesome and anxious period of work for the book. When I stopped to think about why this should be, then I had to admit to my own fears of cultural (Shakespearean) inadequacy. As I do not specialise in Shakespearean scholarship, or have connections with the RSC, and so on, then how could I possibly write anything at all on *the* canonical of canonicals? After several bouts of worry and several drafts of abandoned ideas, I came to the conclusion that sharing such anxieties was a good place to begin resistant performance work.

In your groups, therefore, one of the first tasks you might like to undertake is a shared discussion of Shakespeare the cultural 'giant' and how this makes you feel. To focus your discussion, try addressing two specific contexts: (1) Shakespeare in education; and (2) Shakespeare in performance. Let us think briefly about these two contexts.

Shakespeare in education

Despite the 1980s explosion in critical theory, Shakespeare, as a canonical writer, possibly for many *the* canonical writer, is frequently still taught uncritically, as someone whose work is to be admired and applauded for its beautiful language and 'universal' address: Shakespeare 'speaks' to us all. As Kim F. Hall states:

> Somehow the assumption is that a canonical author must come with a canonized, 'apolitical' formalist reading based in a largely unarticulated project of 'appreciation' which the author cannot exist without. To diverge from the reading is thus to nullify the author. The study of Shakespeare, above all, is supposed to provide a safe haven where we can rise above cultural and critical conflict over difference and revel in our common humanity and love of language.
>
> (Hall 1995: 58–9)

Think about this in relation to how Shakespeare was taught at school. Were you expected to admire his work uncritically? Were you offered the 'common humanity' approach? Like Spence, were you able to 'pass' successfully on the outside as someone capable of 'appreciation', while inside feeling anxiously alienated by dramatic texts you felt you could not fully understand, appreciate or relate to?

And for women especially, how did and do you 'appreciate' the world of the tragic 'heroes', who variously murder wives (Othello), drive their girlfriends mad (Hamlet) or punish their innocent daughters (Lear)? As a resisting critic and performer, you need to think about challenging the 'safe haven' of language appreciation and commonality and to work at 'cultural', 'critical' and gender difference.

Shakespeare in performance

Feminist Renaissance scholar Lisa Jardine has publicly announced her unwillingness to attend any future productions of *King Lear*:

> I have decided I can never again sit through a production of *King Lear*....I don't think this disgraceful reluctance on my part to embark on the emotional marathon which is *King Lear* is entirely my fault. Our great theatre companies have lost their nerve with Shakespeare. The dead hand of compulsory Shakespeare in the National Curriculum means that directors are intimidated by the Bard even before the first read-through with their cast.
>
> (L. Jardine 'The view from here', *Independent*, 24 April 1997, p. 3)

Jardine goes on to describe the work of 'our national theatre companies' as offering 'inert, elitist, studiedly authentic pieces of literary history based on some kind of assumption that audiences 'ought' to enjoy them' (*Ibid.*).

It is important that your group is allowed space to discuss the 'dead hand' of Shakespeare: to discuss experiences of Shakespeare in performance that have made you feel like never seeing another Shakespearean production. Rather than feeling culturally lacking in some way for feeling like this, take up the position of the resisting feminist critic and, moving beyond broad-based discussions of poor aesthetics or production values, think specifically about issues such as gender representation, agency and action, which may have contributed to your reaction. Above all, discuss in your group why, if Shakespeare is claimed as 'universal' and relevant to us all (allegedly irrespective of race, gender or class), does he often seem so dull, alienating and irrelevant? On the other hand, there may also be more pleasurable experiences to recall. Not all productions are directed from the 'universal' viewpoint, just as not all Shakespeare is taught by the school of uncritical appreciation. Alternative performance approaches have focused on ways of producing Shakespeare to make his work more relevant to modern audiences (see Gay 1994: 6). Jardine, for example, contrasts her reaction to the idea of seeing future 'dead hand' productions of *King Lear* with the experience of seeing and enjoying Baz Luhrmann's movie of *Romeo and Juliet* (1996) whose 'fresh, fast and funky' style brought Shakespeare's play alive for her 12-year-old son.

That said, you might still feel the need to discuss just how far the modernising impulse addresses gender issues. Use this brief extract from Penny Gay's *As She Likes It*, commenting on the gender-bias of the RSC, to think further about Shakespeare and the gender and performance issue:

> The result of institutionalisation as a 'flagship' of British culture is that the RSC has become the principal embodiment of the 'Shakespeare myth', the notion that 'Shakespeare' represents the spirit of England itself...that in his works all that is spiritually necessary for us is already spoken. This is clearly a dangerous situation, reinforcing the patriarchal status quo for anyone – especially a woman – working in theatre with the hope of changing society for the better through theatre's playful transgression. It breeds an unconscious assumption that only patriarchal males can truly interpret the Shakespearean text (the priest and Bible syndrome) – a text which is already imbued with patriarchal attitudes which might more profitably be deconstructed.
>
> (Gay 1994: 7–8)

While the organisation of our national Shakespeare company mirrors the male domination of 'the general cultural situation' (*Ibid.*: 10), you are unlikely to see a radical gender shift in Shakespearean performance, and you may well find the 'pleasure' of spectating as a resistant feminist critic has it limits.

In the workshop, however, you have the freedom to make a more radical intervention. Think, for a moment, about Gay's observations on deconstruction and women's 'playful transgression' linked to political change, in relation to Spence who saw her photographic sniping as a deconstructive or transgressive project:

> If my work is about deconstructing visual signs and symbols, it is also concerned with the continual reconstruction of such signs in ways which are more in the interests of those they signify than those who traditionally control signs' production and circulation. Such work is a form of cultural sniping.
>
> (Spence 1995: 135)

My proposal to you is that whereas you may not be able to see professional Shakespearean productions that effect a radical transformation of power away from the male domination of the high-cultural (re)-production, you may effect a more radical redistribution of power and re-circulation of sign-systems through a resistant style of workshopping.

The 'universal' Shakespeare whom we 'ought' to enjoy, as Jardine described, contrasts sharply with the exciting ways that we might find to work as resisting critics and performers who intervene theatrically and politically to disturb the 'master' text. But how to begin? Given all the scholarship on and productions of Shakespeare, this is a difficulty facing any performance group (whether resistant or not). Here are a few proposals to get you into a mode of resistant cultural thinking and practice.

Feminist research to feminist performance

To resist the canonical values of a 'master' text you need to research and to develop an understanding of its cultural–materialist history. With this in mind, try the following research-to-practice suggestions with the help of your dramaturg/s.

Material and cultural re-production

•   Encourage your dramaturg and group to look for past programmes of *King Lear* productions. Have a look through these to see what kinds of framing materials are included. Often, you may find a selection of past commentaries from critical voices that adopt a masculinist position. Have a look at these and think about setting out an alternative selection of extracts from feminist criticisms.

- You might also look for other publicity materials, posters for example, and see how certain images are selected to promote a production. Try critiquing these with extracts from feminist criticisms overlaid on the images. You could also use these materials for physical, image work on the dramatic text.

- Invite your dramaturg to research images of different performances of *King Lear* to help the group towards an understanding of the play's material and cultural production history. It might be particularly useful if you were able to put together a series of images that visually traced the playing of one particular scene and its re-production of gender hierarchies. Who has the status, or is the focus, and how is this encoded, and so on?

- Or, try and trace a visual production history of specific stage roles in relation to gender stereotyping. Find out, for example, how Goneril and Regan were imaged by actresses on the nineteenth-century stage and relate this to women's social and cultural position in the nineteenth century. You could try creating your own 'gallery' out of these images and using them for physical work in relation to the dramatic text.

- You might also try tracing a play's reviewing history. Remember, as Gay points out, 'male intellectuals tend to believe they have special access to the true meaning of Shakespeare's plays', and advises that the historian, especially the feminist historian, 'has to learn to read between the lines' (Gay 1994: 11). Looking at a cross-section of reviews can show you how impossible the definitive, 'true meaning' quest is. You could playfully exploit this by combining commentaries with the acting out of several versions of the 'true meaning' of a particular scene.

- Try getting hold of 'classic' Shakespearean performances on video. Select scenes for viewing. Use 'stop' and 'play' facilities to interrupt viewings with readings from feminist criticisms that resist the dominant, masculine aesthetic. For example, you might select a clip that is played and interrupted with extracts from Sue-Ellen Case's chapter on 'new poetics' (Case 1988), giving details of the gender-bias in dominant traditions of blocking, staging, lighting and so on.

- Group members could be encouraged to go and see a current production of your 'master' play. As feminist critics your group should think about: the venue (its location, social and cultural status); the performers (are they stars, household names, amateur enthusiasts?); playing style (in relation to agency, action and gender); the production values of the performance – the design, the costuming, the use of technical elements; and so on. If you put together your own review commentaries along these lines, you could then try a critical acting out of these: a performance lecture in which you feed back your comments and reactions to the group with visual en-actments.

Re-directions

As you begin to understand your play's cultural and material production history, then you can pursue your research-into-performance explorations to re-direct, open up and resist the dominant (masculine) tradition of playing.

* Try going back to Shakespeare's sources and play with these as counterpoints to the dramatic text. Use them especially to interrogate key moments of dramatic action that are conventionally presented as inevitable and closed. With *King Lear*, for example, look at the alternative folk-tale endings in which Cordelia does not die – not to propose that one is 'better' than another, but to open up, rather than to close down, the dramatic text.
* Use close, feminist readings of particular scenes as instructions for re-directing traditional stagings. Try Kathleen McLuskie's essay on *King Lear* (McLuskie 1985), for example. You might try transposing the 'stop-and-play' video idea into your playing, moving the action and freezing it against feminist readings.
* Invite your dramaturg to bring feminist research into the social conditions for Renaissance women to your group and try inserting this material into the playing of a scene (see Aughterson 1995). What happens, for example, if you frame Cordelia's silence in the opening scene against Lisa Jardine's feminist analysis of Renaissance women and speech (Jardine 1983)?
* You might also consider researching modern feminist issues. For example, your dramaturg might bring current feminist research into elder abuse back to a group working on *King Lear*. How the trials of being long-term carers for elderly relatives causes carers to abuse those in their care, for example, could be used not to reclaim or make a plea for Goneril and Regan, but to resist a

playing of Act II, which insists on a wronged father and 'evil' daughters.

• Try playing a scene that not only inserts the voice of the male reviewer (as above), but also creates a space for the resistant presence of the feminist critic.

From the personal to the political Shakespeare

Directing *King Lear* for the Leicester Haymarket in 1997, which controversially starred Kathryn Hunter in the role of Lear (see later), Helena Kaut-Howson stated: 'We had to decide: what is our way in? We needed a starting point. It is like a massive stone: cut a path in and you reveal things; cut a different one and you reveal others' (Quoted in H. Neill, 'Woman who would be king', *The Times* 18 February 1997, p. 34). Kaut-Howson found her way in by rooting/routing her direction for the play in and through a personal experience. Heather Neill's pre-production preview for *The Times* explains:

> There was, in fact, a highly personal and emotional starting point...[Kaut-Howson's] mother died about eight months ago. 'Her preoccupations were the same as Lear's obsessions: what makes humanity devour itself? What causes wars? She had lived through wars in Europe and the Middle East. At the end she was still herself, as Lear is still himself, only more so.
>
> (*Ibid.*)

Working from personal experience offers you not only a way in to the text, but also a way of resisting the 'here are the important, universal themes and messages in this play that you *ought* to address' approach. Moreover, as life experiences are conditioned by factors such as gender, nationality, race and class, we should think of the personal not just as the 'text' of an individual in isolation but produced by her or his social, cultural and material environment.

Consider this second example, which comes from a mature student who had to deal with her mother's onset of dementia while studying *King Lear* at the Open University:

> At that time, my elderly mother had been causing my two sisters and I a great deal of stress due to her many unreasonable and

frequent demands, with phone calls which could number as many as twenty two in one day. Our relationship had always been fraught and she used to play one daughter off against another in the same way as Lear. Consequently, while reading *Lear* I could not help but identify with the predicament in which Goneril and Regan found themselves. I felt I understood exactly how their aged father made them feel....Now my mother is in a residential home and I know that the dementia problems she was experiencing actually exacerbated the characteristics of a difficult personality. Although I find I can't be entirely supportive of my mother's (Lear's) position, time, freedom from the stress of the situation, and my diminishing guilt, have made me more understanding of her/his fears, her/his need for outward signs of love and gratitude from her/his offspring.

(Ankers 1997; see p. 215)

This personal reaction raises all sorts of social issues: about familial love, duty, responsibility; about how and who cares for elderly parents, and, in particular, the implications for daughters as 'natural' carers. It offers you a resistant way in to working on the text, which you might try and take in the following sorts of practical directions.

- Kaut-Howson used her personal experience to create a frame play for her production, and introduced a *Casualty*-style modern hospital-setting to stage Lear's final hours, which subsequently punctuated the stage action and brought the performance to a close. Try creating your own framing images based on personal experiences you are bringing to the text. These can also provide starting points for alternative plays (see later).
- Develop simple monologues based on your personal experiences and set these against particular lines in the play where you feel they engage critically with the ideological work of the text. For example, if you encouraged your group to share narratives about the care of elderly parents and grandparents, you could develop a monologue for Cordelia as an aside to Lear's lines 'I loved her most, and thought to set my rest/ On her kind nursery' (I. i. 125–6). Have Cordelia speak the lines back to Lear, and then improvise her reaction. Or, work them into responses for Regan and Goneril at the close of I. i. as reactions to the thought of

having a turn and turn-about system of caring for an ageing parent.

• As an alternative to speech-based monologues, repeat the above but encode reactions in a visual, physical text as a counterpoint to verbal cues from the dramatic text.

'Talking heads'

> Shakespeare used to frighten the wits out of me because I was too reverent about it; I didn't smile because I thought that would be wrong. I approached each speech as a 'speech', and I looked at the syntax and the verbal shapes, and as a result I was one of the most boring Shakespearean actors in the world.
>
> (Sinead Cusack, quoted in Rutter and Evans 1988: 54)

Anyone who has had to work at 'speaking' Shakespeare – perhaps as an audition piece, as a reading or in a performance – will probably identify with Sinead Cusack's feeling of being frightened out of her wits. Reverence for the words of the 'bard' can often turn performers into 'talking heads', (acting from the neck upwards), or make it almost impossible to 'speak' at all. Approaches to 'speaking' Shakespeare based on language appreciation and the 'universality' of the Bard (see Werner 1996 on this point), are likely to make you a 'talking head' or a silenced victim of his words. Again, do not be afraid to discuss and to share these sorts of fears and experiences with your group.

Emblem and voice

Most importantly, however, you need to explore ways of empowering your voices. Cusack goes on to reveal how she overcame her particular difficulties when playing Olivia in *Twelfth Night*, and she found herself talking rather than making speeches: 'since then I've never dared approach a text in the analytical way I used to, in case I slip back. Now I only look for a woman' (quoted in Rutter and Evans 1988: 54). This, however, leaves the feminist performer with the problem of 'look[ing]' for the male-identified object she desires to resist.

Instead, taking Cordelia as our working example, try having two women to represent her: the one constructed as a silent emblem of the dutiful daughter, the other empowered to speak. Use the emblematic Cordelia as the vehicle for the social, cultural and theatrical systems that 'fix' her as the pious, virtuous daughter. Use your own feminist responses to the emblem of dutiful daughter to encourage your second Cordelia to speak.

As the speaking Cordelia, do not try to make 'beautiful' speeches, or to intellectualise a response. Then, as you go back to the dramatic text, try to hold on to your own voice, your own responses, as you explore Cordelia's lines. Work slowly through the lines, feeling your way, finding out what is there rather than starting from a position of 'knowing'. Look at the 'fixed' representation of Cordelia/yourself and allow yourself to respond to the silent emblem. See how this 'troubles' the lines; 'troubles' the emblem. Allow the voice to come from inside out, rather than outside in: a voice that comes from inside you as you approach the lines, and not from your culturally received image of Cordelia, which is frozen in another part of the stage.

You can try this again using several bodies to create your emblem, and a chorus of Cordelias. You can quickly achieve a group effect by getting women to work with key lines from personal responses, mixed with key lines from the dramatic text.

Image and voice

Additionally, finding a voice may also connect with finding an image for your role. The actresses in *Clamorous Voices* talk variously about the ways in which they have had to resist the male direction of their character's appearance and costuming. Sinead Cusack, for example, argued with director Adrian Noble for her 1986 Lady Macbeth to be dressed in white rather than black, and eventually had to compromise on green (see Rutter and Evans 1988: 57).

On the other hand, Kaut-Howson empowered her *King Lear* ensemble by allowing the performers to develop their own ideas of what their characters should look like; to make their own decisions (assisted by the designer) about costuming. That both the director and designer were supportive of this, contrasts with the traditional method of director and designers requiring a performer to fit their concept.

So, as you thread your own way through a character, find your own ideas about what she looks like, and negotiate these with the rest of your group. Don't be conditioned by dominant images (look back at your research 'gallery' to remind yourselves). Try working with one or two clothing props that *you* feel are right for the role.

You can also try working on a role 'costumed' with an item of clothing from your own wardrobe. This allows you to keep a sense of your (resistant) self in the role. In contrast to Cusack's experience, for example, Jude Winter describes her workshopping of Lady Macbeth on a Gaulier course where she was encouraged to play Lady Macbeth in her own leather jacket:

> Gaulier did it from the inside, asking how would I show off my leather jacket. (My leather jacket is my prized possession.) And there is a way of showing off my leather jacket, and superimposing that on Lady Macbeth, so that everyone could see the truthfulness of 'me' coming out. It had nothing to do with 'getting into character'; it was a new door – it allowed me to find a truthfulness in representation.
>
> (Siren 1997: 87)

If you think back to the Cordelia example, then working in this way may help you not to get lost in the image of Cordelia as dutiful daughter, and not to lose the resistant voice/self explored in the emblem work.

The words that are not there

One of the frustrations for the feminist reader, critic and performer of Shakespeare is the 'silencing' of the female roles. Fiona Shaw, talking to Carol Rutter about playing Kate in *The Taming of the Shrew*, could explain how she saw Kate as 'somebody whose identity is linked to her behaviour', but added that 'the problem with expressing any of this is that Kate doesn't have the language, she doesn't have the lines' (quoted in Rutter and Evans 1988: 8). In response to those who were critical of her Kate for not 'putting up more of a fight', she argued 'I'm dying to put up a fight but look at the text – it ain't there!' (*Ibid.*: 10). However, the relative freedom of the workshop (as compared to the professional production context), offers you the opportunity to 'put up more of a fight'; to devise your own 'text' for the silenced women.

Lorraine Helms raises interesting points about the linguistic disempowerment of Shakespeare's female characters. Working through Robert Weimann's *Shakespeare and the Popular Tradition*, she refers to the survival of the medieval conventions of *locus* (to designate fictional spaces) and *platea* (as the abstract, non-representational playing space) in the Elizabethan theatre (Helms 1994: 110). She notes: (1) the tradition of direct address from the *platea*, the technique of 'playing the crowd' as practised by the Shakespearean clown and 'clownish' figures; and (2) the evolution of the 'soliloquizing player' who 'moves between *locus* and *platea*', empowered to 'create a dramatic fiction or comment on the theatrical occasion...construct an illusion of interiority or play the crowd' (*Ibid.*: 110–11). Helms develops her analysis of space and speech in relation to gender:

> With some exceptions, Shakespeare's female characters play their roles in the illusionistic scenes of the *locus*. They enjoy few opportunities to express the interiority of the reflexive soliloquy and even fewer to address the audience from the interactive *platea*.
>
> (*Ibid.*: 111)

In the workshop, however, you can empower the women characters with 'opportunities' for both interiority and direct address. You can experiment with what Cordelia may wish to say directly to us, or indirectly as she ponders her 'private' thoughts.

Uncensored speeches of incensed women

For further ideas on monologue-making, and as a useful point of reference for this kind of devising in a Shakespearean context, have a look at Christine Brückner's 'Desdemona – if you had only spoken!', the title monologue in a collection of 'eleven uncensored speeches of eleven incensed women', translated by actress Eleanor Bron (Brückner 1992 [1983]). The Desdemona monologue is a poignant, angry and witty admonishment of the Fieldmarshal who puts his 'trust in a scrap of stuff that is used for blowing one's nose, or mopping one's brow, or even to wipe away tears' (1992: 116). Bron explains the impulse for the monologues in Brückner's collection:

> All these women had things to say that they had never yet had the chance to say, and they had had enough of their enforced silence: they were all angry. In any rehearsal or acting workshop there is one crucial question which crops up over and over again: *Why* does this person speak now? The answer to the question provides the energy that gives the character life. The entire

premise of Christine Brückner's book was each woman's urgent
need to speak out, at last, now.

(Bron 1992: xii)

You can break the 'enforced silence' of different women characters in
Shakespeare through devising your own monologues and seeing
what follows as you focus on 'each woman's urgent need to speak
out'. Your group can experiment with setting your devised monologues against scenes played 'straight' from the dramatic text. Try
freezing the general action in the *locus*, but free-up your women
characters with movement and speech.

Cross-gender playing

Cross-gender playing is a way of giving women performers access to
the male roles (see also the cross-gender section in Chapter 4). Cross-
gendered productions in the 1990s where women have taken the
male leads have tended not to exploit the gap between the woman
performer and the masculine role. Kathryn Hunter approached Lear,
for example, as 'an old man – definitely not Queen Lear – but
without overcharacterising age or gender' (H. Neill, 'Woman who
would be king', *The Times* 18 February 1997, p. 34). Director
Deborah Warner noted how her casting of Fiona Shaw as Richard II
in the Cottesloe production (1995) began with a gap, 'the discrep-
ancy, the awkwardness' between gender and role, which the cast, and
subsequently, audiences, closed down through acceptance, rather than
opening up through complex negotiation and questioning (Warner
1996: 233). That said, in your own workshopping, you may find that
playfully exploiting the gap helps to make visible gender lines that
are usually concealed. As Alisa Solomon comments on audience reaction to a cross-gendered *Lear*:

> Accepting the facts on the stage, as any engaged spectator even-
> tually must, the audience takes in a world where the matriarch
> presides. But they are still faced with seeing familiar relationships
> and events made strange. Even a spectator with no previous
> knowledge of *Lear* brings assumptions of a patriarchal culture
> that make the production disjunctive and discomfiting. Nowhere
> is this effect more striking than in the new intensity of the play's
> relentless violence.
>
> (Solomon 1997: 139)

Here are some suggestions for cross-gendered play.

- Be aware of cross-gendered linguistic play and action. What happens to Lear's 'And let not women's weapons, water drops,/ Stain my man's cheeks' (II. iv. 276–7) when they are spoken by a woman in the role?
- Look at how the visual, physical text of a woman in a man's role en-genders the playing. Hunter, who has been described as a 'tiny, smoky-voiced' actress (S. Hemming 'Friday on her mind', *Observer*, Review Section, 3 March 1996, p. 12) in the role of Lear seemed, at times, like an ancient spirit or child, and when cursing Goneril's womb in I. iv., for example, her Lear gave a visual presence to the unborn child of the womb-cursed-daughter.
- To highlight how dominant culture and traditions of playing are ideologically loaded against women, invite your dramaturg to research (male) reviewing of female Hamlets or Lears, and punctuate the cross-gendered playing of a scene with these. Use your playing to critique and upstage the reviews. You could try working with historical accounts (Sarah Bernhardt's Hamlet, for example), and/or focus on contemporary productions, such as Hunter's Lear, which attract wide newspaper coverage.
- As all of Shakespeare's roles for women were originally written to be played by men, what happens if you try and play a male role as a woman, playing a man, playing a woman? Try a Brechtian register in which you show your audiences that you are women 'putting on' men's roles, to play (man-made) representations of women. Don't try for realism – keep showing the 'gaps'.
- In her essay 'Acts of Resistance', Lorraine Helms discusses femininity and clowning, and considers the possibility of 'a Shakespearean stage on which a woman may play the clown' (Helms 1994: 130). With this in mind, try developing the role of the fool into a cultural sniper: make him a woman, and allow her to improvise commentaries on the action that she speaks directly to the audience (see later on *Lear's Daughters*).
- One final suggestion. Think about the male domination of theatre as a profession, and the male domination of Shakespeare in particular, in relation to your own woman-centred group. Think about how you have to cross over into roles usually occupied by men. Both Hunter and Shaw were partnered by women

directors (with whom they are also friends). Do you feel this might make a difference to working and performance practice/s? (As a follow-up, see Helms on her fantasy of 'The Weyward Sisters' as a concept for a feminist Shakespearean touring company (Helms 1994: 139).)

Alternatives

A number of contemporary playwrights have responded to their own cultural anxieties about Shakespeare by writing their own versions of *Hamlet* or *Lear* (see the Resources section). You may find it helpful, for instance, to look at *Lear's Daughters* by Elaine Feinstein and the Women's Theatre Group (1991), which keeps Lear off-stage and focuses on the three daughters, a nanny and an androgynous fool (played by a woman). The figures of the fool and the nanny offer you examples of female clowning and the empowerment of a traditionally disenfranchised, minor, female figure. As *Lear's Daughters* ends with a freeze-frame image of the three princesses reaching out for a crown, there are ways of playing this image as a frame play for *King Lear* and seeing where this takes you. You may find that workshopping *Lear's Daughters* in tandem with *King Lear* offers you a useful resistant performance strategy, although a more ambitious group might take this as their cue to devise their own alternative to the 'master' text.

One final point to consider in devising your own alternatives to canonical texts is that the workshop context offers you the freedom to experiment and permits you to be as playfully resistant as you like. In professional production contexts, you need to be aware that canonical texts in copyright restrict your freedom to play. The Wooster Group's mid-1980s show *L.S.D. (...Just the High Points...)* was forced to close after Arthur Miller threatened legal action because the piece included sections from *The Crucible*. I feel fairly certain that if you applied some of the cultural-sniping practices suggested in this chapter to a professional production of *Death of a Salesman* or *The Crucible* you would find the production banned! Deborah Warner, for instance, found out just how restricting copyright can be when her West End revival of *Footfalls* (also with Fiona Shaw) was banned by the Beckett Estate, because she transposed two lines and 'failed' to follow the stage directions (Warner 1996: 230).

Shakespeare's work is not protected by copyright, but you will find that his work is professionally restricted by the (patriarchal)

canonical reverence of the 'dead hand' kind. Realistically, therefore, in
a professional context you are more likely to find that you take on
the role of resistant, feminist performer, rather than be able to make a
whole production feminist (see the interviews in Rutter and Evans
1988). The resistant theatrical practice of 'cultural sniping' arms you
for a feminist attack, rather than a cultural revolution.

'Cultural sniping': summary checklist

- Your group need to be allowed space to share their anxieties
  about a 'master' text that may have a gender, class or race (or
  combination of these) base.
- To research your 'canonical' text, take on the role of resistant
  feminist critic.
- Work with your materials (academic and/or personal) to re-
  present the dominant ideology, aesthetic and playing history of
  your 'master' text.
- Aim to keep hold of a resistant voice.
- Aim for a performance register that is broadly Brechtian: one in
  which it is clear that you are 'putting on' or 'trying out' roles;
  playing with them, but not getting 'inside' them.
- Try devised 'alternatives' – whether monologues, scenes, or
  complete pieces – in tandem with the 'master' text.
- If you are going to show your work (e.g. a workshop presentation) then think about the social and cultural status of your
  venue.
- If you publicise your work, then design publicity materials
  (programmes/posters) that draw attention to your cultural
  sniping.
- If possible, have a post-presentation discussion with your spectators and take them through your resistant practice.

RESOURCES

The field of Shakespearean scholarship is vast and overwhelming, so
suggestions here are a tiny fraction of what is available to you. What I
would advise is that your dramaturg thinks carefully about the kinds
of materials most useful to your group. These are likely to be those

that make use of feminism and/or cultural-materialism, and pay attention to the performance (as opposed to literary) context. For getting started, Sinfield's two essay contributions to *Political Shakespeare* are useful for discussions on the cultural and educational role of Shakespeare: 'Give an account of Shakespeare and Education, showing why you think they are effective and what you have appreciated about them. Support your comments with precise references' and 'Royal Shakespeare: Theatre and the Making of Ideology' (in (Dollimore and Sinfield, 1985).

Aughterson's sourcebook (1995) is good for documents you might introduce into workshopping women and the Renaissance. For feminist scholarship on Renaissance drama, culture and society try Jardine (1983), and C. Belsey *The Subject of Tragedy* (London and New York: Routledge, 1985). McLuskie (1985) is also particularly useful for re-directing *King Lear*, and Solomon's account of the Mabou Mines cross-gendered *Lear* is also instructive (Solomon 1997: 130–44).

The interviews with RSC actresses in Rutter and Evans (1988) offer you very useful insights into the difficulties for the feminist performer working on Shakespeare in the mainstream, and Werner (1996) is an insightful feminist critique of voice-training methods and playing Shakespeare. Gay (1994) also has useful commentaries for the feminist performer in Shakespeare's comedies, and Helms (1994) shows the uses of feminist history for the contemporary 'feminist player'. Donkin and Clement (1993) include a section on subverting the 'classics' – in particular, try Gay Gibson Cima's list of practical suggestions for subverting the canon (Cima 1993).

Modern alternatives to *King Lear* include Edward Bond's *Lear* (London: Methuen, 1978); Barrie Keeffe's *King of England* (London: Methuen, 1980); Adrian Mitchell's *The Tragedy of King Real* (London: Methuen, 1985); Howard Barker's *Seven Lears* (London: John Calder, 1990); and *Lear's Daughters* by the Women's Theatre Group and Elaine Feinstein, in E. Aston and G. Griffith (eds) *Herstory: Volume 1* (Sheffield: Sheffield Academic Press, 1991). *Lear's Daughters* is of most direct relevance to feminist playing, but Keefe's *King of England* also raises race, class, gender and health care issues, through his Black, retiring British railway worker, Mr King, whose daughter, Susan, works as a nurse in an ailing National Health System.

Also of interest is Siren's parody of the *Hamlet* ghost sequence in *Now Wash Your Hands Please* published in T. Fairbanks *Pulp and Other Plays* (Amsterdam: Harwood, 1996), and *Gertrude and Ophelia* and *Good Night Desdemona (Good Morning Juliet)* by Canadian playwrights

Margaret Clarke and Ann-Marie MacDonald, respectively. Extracts from these two plays appear in C. Zimmerman (ed.) *Taking the Stage* (Toronto: Playwrights Canada Press, 1994). In particular, MacDonald's comic creation of a woman lecturer who proposes Shakespeare's tragedies are comedies and enters the dramatic world of *Othello* offers you a lively and imaginative example of how you might work the figure of the feminist critic into an entertaining, resistant practice.

For further examples of feminist monologues devised from canonical texts, try Franca Rame's one-woman *Medea* in D. Fo and F. Rame, *Female Parts One Woman Plays* (London: Pluto Press, 1981), and Brückner's monologue for Clytaemnestra (Brückner 1992 [1983]).

Chapter 6

Past tense, present tense

In Chapter 5 we examined ways of challenging the canon through feminist performance. We noted that not only does a feminist approach to theatre require that we study and perform canonical texts differently, or rather, deconstructively as resistant performers, but that it is also necessary to look beyond the canon to that which history and theatre history has marginalised. The aim of this chapter is to concentrate on the 'margins' where so much of women's work has been 'lost' to view and recovered through feminist research. Note that the concerns of these two chapters are by no means discrete: the margins are created through the making of the canon. The reader may find it useful, therefore, to cross-reference theory and practice in these two chapters, and to try out practical suggestions in this chapter on canonical texts, and vice versa.

The particular focus for this chapter is realism. I selected this as the vehicle for illustrating the kinds of formal, ideological and practical problems we need to consider when reviving 'lost' women's theatre from a past stage, because it is such a controversial dramatic form within the feminist theatre academy. Issues raised by historians, theorists and practitioners in relation to realism help, however, in our understanding of the kinds of questions we need to ask when trying to play the past in a subversive present tense.

In order to explore the issues of realism for the feminist performer, I propose to use three late nineteenth- and early twentieth-century plays by women: *Alan's Wife* (1893) by Florence Bell and Elizabeth Robins, *Chains* (1909) by Elizabeth Baker, and *Rutherford and Son* (1912) by Githa Sowerby, collected in *New Woman Plays* (Fitzsimmons and Gardner 1991). All three plays have recourse to realism in their authorship; all three have been canonically marginalised and only recently recovered through feminist theatre scholarship.

Feminism and realism

The dangers

In the opening chapter I touched briefly on the ways in which realist traditions of stage drama and the Method-acting style associated with it have been attacked by many feminists as being oppressive to women. The feminist attack stems from a perception of realism as a conservative dramatic form, reflecting, reproducing and reinforcing dominant ideology. Catherine Belsey's work on classic realism provides a seminal reference point for this view:

> The work of ideology is to represent the position of the subject as fixed and unchangeable, an element in a given system of differences which is human nature and the world of human experience, and to show possible action as an endless repetition of 'normal', familiar action. To the extent that the classic realist text performs this work, classic realism is an ideological practice.
>
> (Belsey 1980: 90)

Defining realism is by no means a straightforward critical task (see Schroeder 1996: Chapter 1), although formally and ideologically it is commonly identified by its 'closed' operations of character, action and narrative organisation (see later), which attempt to fix the 'normal' or 'familiar' in the interests of social stability and the *status quo*. It is realism's 'endless repetition' of women 'fixed' in dominant heteropatriarchal systems of representation that has fuelled the feminist attack.

To think about these dangers, an early group discussion should be organised to see how individual group members feel about dramatic realism and the representation of women. As a talking point you may find this extract from Gillian Hanna's 1978 interview useful. Discussing Monstrous Regiment's production of *Vinegar Tom* (Caryl Churchill), Hanna thinks through the (male-identified) concept of a 'traditional play' with 'naturalistic scenes' and her feminist desire to 'smash' this 'regular and acceptable theatrical form':

The form of *Vinegar Tom* was extremely bizarre. You had a series of quite naturalistic scenes punctuated by very modern songs in modern dress. It all came to some kind of conclusion, and then at the end you had two music hall characters coming out of the blue, developing it nowhere. If you took out the music you would have something akin to a traditional play. But we knew that we had to have the music to smash that regular and acceptable theatrical form. We didn't sit down and say deliberately that we needed to smash that form, but that is what we did none the less; I think we unconsciously felt a need to do that. As a feminist, I think it also has to do with feeling that you are running, acting, moving counter to the prevailing culture.

(Hanna 1978: 9)

Discuss in your group whether you are starting with a sense that it is possible to be represented in a dominant, 'traditional' play, such as a realist drama, or whether, like Hanna, you feel the need to 'smash that form'.

Your group should think about 'traditional' realist plays they have seen and think back to how the women characters were represented and what part they played in the narrative structure.

The possibilities

While the dangers that the formal and ideological properties of realism may represent for women have been hotly argued by some feminists, realism also has its defenders within the feminist academy. As Dolan explains, views on realism will vary according to different feminist positions: 'liberal feminists, and women who argue against the need for establishing new dramatic forms, find nothing to fault in the traditional well-made play and the psychological acting practices that give it voice' (Dolan 1988: 84).

Theatre historian Sheila Stowell, for example, makes a feminist case for realism in the context of British suffrage drama. Taking issue with Dolan *et al.* for the feminist attacks on realism, Stowell argues that women playwrights from this period brought a radical edge to this conservative form through using 'realism's recognisable worlds' to challenge rather than to reinforce 'normative ideology' (Stowell 1992a: 100). Working on the woman-authored dramatic text in the social and cultural context of Edwardian theatre, Stowell makes a persuasive case for 'rehabilitating realism' in its moment of feminist theatre history (Stowell 1992b). Patricia Schroeder also outlines compelling arguments for looking at *The Feminist Possibilities of Dramatic Realism* in different historical moments in the twentieth-century tradition of 'feminist realists' writing for the American stage – most especially in respect of African–American women writers (Schroeder 1996: 9).

In short, you need to be prepared to think about both of these points of view – the dangers and the possibilities. Perhaps most importantly, however, the feminist performer needs to think beyond the 'feminist possibilities of *dramatic* realism', to the consequences of realism in performance. If it is possible to argue the subversive potential of woman-authored Edwardian, realist drama at the level of the dramatic text (see next section), how is the feminist performer, working in a theatrical, realist frame to realise that potential? Can she find a way of playing the past in a subversive present tense? Can she find a feminist performance register to activate the 'lost' woman-authored realist script?

When interviewed by Michelene Wandor, company members of Mrs Worthington's Daughters, a group committed to 'resurrect[ing] plays from the past', explained that in their view recovering women's plays was a way of demonstrating that women could be just as good as men: 'we'd shown that there were very competent women play-wrights who were the equivalents of the male writers of their time' (Wandor, interview, 1983: 21). The company then went on to comment on the difficulties that they had encountered in 'finding material that steps out of its period enough to remain interesting to a modern audience' (*Ibid.*).

However, I would urge you to think differently about your feminist aims and objectives in a feminist recovery project. Aiming to resurrect a play and to perform it to prove that women were as competent as men at writing realism or any other dramatic form does not in itself constitute a feminist performance. Neither, I would suggest, can the modern feminist performer rely on seeking out the past that might be of interest to the present, but must look to ways in which she can intervene in the text to make it speak to us in a subversive present tense. If the Edwardian woman writer was able to encode a feminist possibility in her dramatic text, then the modern feminist practitioner needs to explore ways of realising that possibility in her performance. In brief, what I am proposing is a practical exploration that explores or negotiates the 'feminist possibilities of dramatic realism' through a materialist–feminist theatre practice.

Dramatic 'keys' to feminist performance

Stowell's analysis of suffrage theatre (Stowell 1992a) centres on close textual readings of the plays with a focus on genre. You may find the critical, close-reading practice useful in the research-to-practice stage of a potential project. A shared group study of generic conventions governing realism can help you to find dramatic 'keys' out of which to develop a materialist–feminist performance register (see later).

Your group could try a brainstorming session in which members bring in examples of realist drama from the late nineteenth century. The dramaturg could be invited to co-ordinate this activity. Find out which characteristics you can agree on as a basic working model or pattern for dramatic realism. Remember that there is no single definition of dramatic realism, but devising a particular scheme for practical work can help raise awareness in your group of the formal conventions (and the dangers) of their signifying practices. At the risk of oversimplification, here is a four-part proposal to provide an example:

1   A linear, 'closed' narrative and structural organisation through which dominant values may be critiqued but reinstated in the resolution of action.
2   Agency that positions the masculine as subject and initiator of action/s and expels its (feminine) transgressors.
3   A linguistic sign-system that operates according to the laws and logic of the symbolic order.
4   A fictional world focused (mostly, although not exclusively) on the 'real' domestic landscape.

Your group could use your working model to look at 'lost' plays by women in the realist tradition that you are thinking of working on, to see whether, at the level of the dramatic text, conventions operate as a formal site of resistance (or not). In the three plays from the *New Woman Plays* collection, you can begin to see patterns of dramatic deviancy. To summarise using the four-part model proposed above:

Alan's Wife

1   Narrative structured into three short scenes that refuse 'closure' because:

2   the principal agent (a woman/mother) refuses to acknowledge infanticide as an act of transgression and
3   retreats from the symbolic into a language of silence expressed through her maternal body in a
4   prison setting, which functions metaphorically as the condemned landscape of the maternal body.

Rutherford and Son

1   Organised in three acts that take the form of a series of familial oppositions to the Father, and effects a critique of the capitalist–patriarch through
2   the agency of his daughter-in-law, Mary Rutherford, which resides largely in her
3   non-verbal presence until the resolution when she speaks the language of the capitalist and successfully bargains for the welfare of her son, the price for which is her
4   continued imprisonment in the domestic landscape.

Chains

1   Organised in four acts which reverse:
2   traditional patterns of agency by placing the capitalist earner of the family wage, Charley Wilson, in the passive, feminine position, from which it proves impossible for
3   the language of action/change to be anything other than empty rhetoric, as the discovery that he is a father-to-be binds him all the more tightly to the
4   oppressive site of waged labour and domesticity.

Dramatic techniques that are used strategically to challenge domestic realism, therefore, are those that we are able to identify as resistant to the linear and linguistic patterns of formal and ideological closure.

You may also find it helpful to further an understanding of the dramatic conventions of realism and techniques of potentially subversive rule-breaking, by looking at a range of representative realist dramas authored by men in the same period. You may then be able to compare and contrast the ideological implications of, for example, the unrepentant female/maternal transgressor in *Alan's Wife* with the transgressor who effects formal and ideological closure through the confession and admission of her sins (typically the 'woman with a past' who features regularly in the popular dramas of Jones and Pinero, for example).

Re-working realism

Another useful form of dramatic study is to look for examples of feminist playwrights or practitioners who may be making use of realism on the modern stage. Again, the dramaturg in your group could be invited to bring examples into the group or to co-ordinate a group search.

Briefly, to offer just one example: the playwright Sarah Daniels frequently writes in a realist mode, but constantly makes use of dramatic and theatrical techniques that challenge its conventions. Typically, Daniels disrupts our expectations of realism by:

* using a contiguous rather than a linear dramatic organisation;
* interrupting the flow of action with a monologue for a disempowered female figure denied linguistic space;
* creating endings that leave the domestic heteropatriarchal landscape for an utopian, 'surreal' fantasy world;
* creating domestic scenes that are women-only;
* breaking the naturalistic fourth wall by multiplying the fictional spaces in the main playing space.

You can use your explorations into the dramatic techniques of realism from the 'lost' plays, or the re-working realism techniques of a modern feminist dramatist like Daniels, to begin practical work. Even if, as Stowell argues, the turn-of-the-century women playwrights were able to manipulate the conventions of realism, a view, which as we have seen, may be supported by dramatic analysis, there is always the danger that in performance the seamless, closed world of realism will be reinstated. Here are some suggestions for extending the dramatic analysis into practical exploration.

Structural organisation

Your group could try playing with the organisation of material in ways that pattern the dramatic action differently. What happens if the prison scene in *Alan's Wife* is used to open the play, and extracts from this scene are used to interrupt and to comment on the action in others?

Your group could devise an opening sequence that refuses to be contained within the 'rules' or conventions of realism. Points of reference that might be useful for this are the opening dinner scene in Churchill's *Top Girls* (see Chapter 7), or the supermarket scene with which Daniels opens *Beside Herself* (Daniels 1994). These scenes bring together women characters from mythical, fictional, historical or biblical contexts in ways that transgress the boundaries of the 'real'.

Alternatively, your group could play with endings by imagining dramatic action beyond the moment of closure. A starting point might be to improvise a 'realistic' scene of Mary and her son ten years after the ending of *Rutherford and Son*, or by acting out a domestic, post-baby scene at the Wilsons in *Chains*. But then try and image these differently. Try playing with the kinds of fantasy utopian endings that Sarah Daniels uses to overturn her domestic landscapes, allowing her women characters the possibility of escape (see, for example, the ending to *Ripen Our Darkness*, Daniels 1991).

Agency

Looking at the formal properties of the Edwardian feminist drama highlights the complexity of agency: 'Alan's Wife' functions as unrepentant female/maternal transgressor; Mary Rutherford initiates the 'silent' rebellion against the patriarch, and Charley Wilson occupies the passive, feminine position, which is denied agency. All three, however, are constrained by the binary framework of masculinity and femininity. The varying degrees of resistance take place within the heteropatriarchal structures that the protagonists challenge, but, ultimately, cannot overturn. Deconstructive workshop play with the gender divide may further an understanding of how characters seeking agency, desiring beyond the structures of the world in which they are framed, are 'blocked'.

For example, it might be useful to play and re-play family scenes from *Rutherford and Son* to stop those patriarchal/capitalist forces, embodied in Rutherford, which seek to uphold the 'truth' and unchangeability of the familial and economic structures, by taking speech away from the 'blocking' character, or by removing him from the playing space altogether. What happens to those characters who desire agency and change if the opposition is silenced or absent? Alternatively, your group could try re-presenting the father-figure as a comic type, using the comic play to heighten awareness of the 'blocking' impulse. It is useful to try switching between the two, between exaggerated, comic 'overplay' and the silenced/absent opposition to see what changes occur and how performers feel moving across both modes.

Or, your group could try playing a family scene from *Chains* based on Boal's forum technique (see p. 46): sculpt a family image and explore what has to change for Charley to be released from the 'feminine' sphere of oppression.

Linguistic 'space'

The silencing of 'blocking' characters, as detailed above, could also work in tandem with creating monologues for the disempowered figures. For example, a monologue could be created for the off-stage, unseen servant figure, Susan, in *Rutherford and Son*, which could be played against one of the father/family opposition sequences. See what happens if the internecine struggles among the family members are interrupted (freeze-framed, perhaps) by a servant's monologue. What kind of critique emerges? What status, gender or class questions are raised?

Try turning the extra-dialogic stage directions into a spoken text. This can create a critical commentary in a number of different ways. For example:

- Introduce the realistic set directions as a verbal text against an empty playing space (i.e. where the dramatic world referred to is 'absent').
- Narrate entrances and exits (to draw attention to who is in the space, points of departure, etc.).
- Interrogate dialogue by using directions for movement and speech in which the performer 'disobeys' the instruction by moving or speaking contrary to the physical or vocal instructions.
- Alternatively, try playing some scenes by using the extra-dialogic stage directions as a set of instructions for actions without words. Use this kind of exploration for looking at gestural patterns, perhaps for individual characters/performers, and for the group ensemble.

Finally, try 'making strange' the ordinary activities and actions of the characters that 'point to' the 'real' world with 'unreal' or 'surreal' actions. Experiment with Lily Wilson in *Chains* serving her husband's dinner with his gardening tools. Or, try Charley working the garden with knives and forks. As Jude Winter comments, it is this kind of 'disrespectful' play with a text that 'is the kind of process which can take the performer on to something else they can really enjoy' (Ramsden and Winter 1994: 128).

Domestic landscape

Find ways of imaging the domestic through the body. If there are gestural patterns for an individual character, for example, is there an 'oppressive text' in the patterning that can be worked into a physical, choreographed ensemble? (See later the section on 'Feminist performance registers' for a development of this idea.)

Try looking through the set directions and making a note of objects that you could use to create a domestic landscape in a stylised rather than a 'realistic' way. See what significance domestic objects might have to different characters (see the exercise on everyday objects in Chapter 8). Moreover, encourage performers to select objects that are not associated with their character, but represent what they desire but cannot have. Take Rutherford away from his pipe or desk, for example, and see how fetishistic play with the child's bonnet can re-direct or impact on the playing and staging of a scene.

The feminist practitioner as cultural historian

In her autobiographical performance-lecture 'Working in the Margin: Women in Theatre History', Jacky Bratton demonstrates through the *Gestus* of juggling (*Gestus* is the act of showing a subject's relation to structures of social control), that practice alone may not be enough to equip the performer in certain kinds of performance contexts. 'Practising juggling', she comments, 'has not actually led me to the answer to the questions I want to ask about it as a cultural historian: such as why the skill that William Hazlitt admired in the Indian jugglers...has become marketable' (Bratton 1994: 123). Bratton's performance-as-theatre-history-lecture serves as a reminder to the practitioner that she may also need to take on the role of cultural historian in her preparation for a performance (see also Chapter 5, p. 88).

Although it may not always be readily accessible, it is helpful to research documentation of past stages in order to develop an understanding of the historical, social, cultural and theatrical production contexts. This is not just, for example, a question of finding out how women were represented on the stage, but how staged images of femininity read inter-textually with the representation of women in other social and cultural texts.

For 'lost' play projects your group will find it useful to appoint a dramaturg to the role of feminist cultural historian. As illustrated in Bratton's history–performance-lecture, the questions that the cultural historian asks about women, about the cultural and material conditions of their creative and social lives, are ones that the feminist practitioner needs to ask and to bring to her performance work.

Social and cultural contexts

As much of Edwardian drama treated aspects of the 'Woman's Question', it would, for instance, be useful to look at relevant social issues such as marriage and divorce laws, attitudes towards motherhood, and so on. Contemporaneous with the performances of *Alan's Wife* (28 April and 2 May 1893), for instance, was a newspaper report on the case of a gas stoker's wife who allegedly, in a state of diminished responsibility, 'killed' her baby by throwing it out of a window (reported in the *Pall Mall Gazette* 2 May 1893, p. 5). This account might be used to foreground the issue of infanticide in *Alan's Wife* (extracts from the newspaper reporting might be played in the 'murder' scene), or could provide a more extensive source of devising, either in relation to the scripted play or, perhaps, as a project in its own right. It is also an idea to think through modern parallels: how are women who 'kill' their children judged today? What language is used to describe them?

One of the benefits of appointing a dramaturg to undertake this kind of research is that it means that one woman can take on primary responsibility for this kind of investigation, and have more time and space, perhaps, for tracking down less accessible and more original materials. Where research activities are restricted by time, there are a number of materials readily available through feminist journals and publishing houses (see the Resources section), which can provide useful 'short-cuts'. In a modern anthology such as *Strong-Minded Women* (Murray 1982), for example, there are sections on women and clerical work (pp. 318–25), and women as shop assistants (pp. 356–61) that could be used to understand and to workshop Mary

Rutherford's past life in a London office, or Maggie's working life as a shop girl in *Chains* (which is referred to, but not shown on stage). Photographic material from the period can also be a useful resource, especially when looking at representations of femininity. As actress Janet Suzman discussing the role of Hedda Gabler comments:

> Looking at photographs of the period can be especially useful. From them you glean more about furnishing, clothes, manners, demeanour, than from any sociological tract. Julia Margaret Cameron's portraits, for example, will tell you more about Victorian women and how they recorded themselves than many a novel.
>
> (Suzman 1980: 86)

Studying how women were constrained by dress, carriage and social etiquette can be used in workshopped exploration of the body. If simple clothing props that imprison or constrain the body are used and a set of movement exercises are repeated, it can be seen how the body is changed or deformed by the restrictions (see also Chapter 4, pp. 66–8).

Jackie Clune details an apposite example of this in her account of a devised performance-project based on the suffragette movement. When throwing stones to smash glass bottles, an exercise set up to explore 'militancy and appropriate behaviour', she describes how her devising group tried to get a sense of what it felt like for the militant suffragettes to be inhibited by Edwardian dress codes, movement and so on, 'by inserting small branches down the back of our clothing to effect that particular upright rigid-backed posture. The discomfort and lack of mobility we experienced was a turning-point in our thinking about the obstacles these women had to overcome in order to be active militants' (Clune 1992: 12–13). Moreover, the *Gestus* of stone throwing was one that was important to the final production, illustrating how this kind of preliminary workshopping can be instrumental in not just working towards but constructing a performance text .

It may also be fruitful to explore the status of women's creativity, or the social standing (or lack of it) of the woman dramatist. Researching biographical details of Elizabeth Robins, Elizabeth Baker or the 'lost' Githa Sowerby (so little is known about her), could help with understanding the gender constraints of the playwriting profession, and, more broadly, perhaps, the constraints upon women seeking careers in other professional spheres. Such research might eventually develop into the kind of devised project discussed in Chapter 9 (particularly in the case of the enigmatic Sowerby).

Theatre research

With regard to theatre research, sources that may prove useful are newspaper reviews, theatre posters, production photographs, publicity photographs of individual performers, theatre programmes, acting manuals and so on. In particular, this material can be looked at with a view to developing an awareness of gender responses. For example, did mainstream (male) newspaper reviewing reflect a gender bias in its commentary? If women commented on a performance (in the suffrage press, for instance), did gender make a difference to how they understood the performance of a play? In production photographs how are actors and actresses staged in relation to each other? How is gender and status encoded in familial groupings?

As with readings of the dramatic text, there are a variety of ways that theatre research can be used to begin practical work. Here is a list of workshop suggestions.

Review sources

Try using review sources as a commentary on performance. Take a review, for example, that comments on a specific scene and use it to interrupt or comment on the scene relevant to the newspaper commentary. If working towards a full-scale production, it might be interesting to have slides made of the review material that could be projected against a performed scene. Where there are reviews available that show a gender difference in reception, try staging this difference by playing and re-playing a scene according to the engendered lines of interpretation.

Try using production commentaries in the practical study of character construction. For example, in Marjorie Strachey's review of *Rutherford and Son* the figure of the patriarch is criticised for its stereotyping of a 'regular stage figure' (Strachey 1912: 219). On the other hand, Janet is discussed as the most interesting character of the play, and Strachey fantasises about a different life for her: 'if only Janet had been brought into Rutherford's when she was a girl, where her powers would have been called out instead of stifled....What a different household that would have been!' (pp. 220–1). Playing

Rutherford as a social type may be one way of critiquing the capitalist–patriarch; developing other 'lives' for Janet may serve as another way into deconstructing the patriarchal text. (Strachey's commentaries might also be delivered alongside character dialogue, as previously suggested.)

Production photographs

Like period photography, production photographs can be very useful to you for exploring visual registers, both for developing feminist performance registers and aesthetics (see next section for further detail). Publicity shots of a 'staged' scene could be recreated as freeze-framed images, and scenes might be explored with a series of still frames interrupting or disrupting the stage action.

Photographic material can be a useful visual vehicle for helping performers to explore acting styles. Melodramatic encodings of social types (the overbearing father, the oppressed wife, mother, daughter, etc.) read from past photographs (or read into them, as these often look 'old-fashioned', artificial, to the modern eye), can be played against more 'realistic' representations as a further way of exploring gender roles and stereotyping.

As with review commentaries, slides of an Edwardian production could be used to counterpoint a style of modern playing, or the playing space. Projected images of the Edwardian 'realistic' set could be used to heighten its past/present artificiality. Publicity portraits of the actresses who played in the original productions might be imaged against the modern performers to question identity, presence, systems of representation, images of femininity and so on.

Feminist performance registers

The theory/practice guidelines set out in this chapter adopt a feminist position that demands that we interrogate rather than accept the formal and ideological constraints of realism. The workshop ideas are all put forward as possible ways of making a feminist intervention in the realistic frame. In this final section I wish to propose thinking about further exploration and development of physical performance registers that open up rather than close down the 'feminist possibilities' of playing realism and may allow us the possibility of seeing beyond the 'Father'.

Ensemble rhythm/s as transgressive playing

The materialist–feminist techniques that have been 'plotted' in this chapter try to exploit the 'gaps' in the 'closed' world of bourgeois realism. Exercises that you set up to develop an acting style, in a workshop, or possibly in working towards a production context, need to find a performance register that signals its resistance to the logos/symbolic through the body of the performer. This could be explored through the development of a transgressive ensemble rhythm. To illustrate what is meant by this and how it might be realised, we can look at developing a rhythm that critiques power and patriarchy in *Rutherford and Son*.

Rutherford and Son offers an interrogation of power within the familial setting, where the father-figure is critiqued not just as the patriarchal head of the family, but also as the capitalist who has responsibility for a 'family' of workers (represented in the figure of Martin). The fictional playing space in *Rutherford and Son* is the space of Rutherford/the father. How characters move in it will demonstrate how they relate to the father (symbolic). From Sowerby's text we can note that: Dick hurries out of it; John hangs in it uncomfortably; Anne wanders through it without purpose; Janet sulks silently in it; Mary stays silently but tenaciously in it; and Martin waits on the threshold of the space that he does not cross unless invited.

Performers can experiment with moving from a neutral mode in a playing space, to taking on a character-designated role in the fictional playing space, on their own, with one other performer/character, and building into the complete ensemble. As each performer/character also takes up a place within the symbolic (perhaps a particular chair, or corner of the room), find out which other characters they allow into it. Try playing status games, switching between high and low status to authorise or to ban the crossing of spatial boundaries. What happens, for example, if Rutherford enters the room as a low-status figure and other family members are given high status? Does this empower them to 'transgress' normal boundaries? Is Rutherford kept out of his space?

The ensemble patterns and rhythms of movement should be encouraged to become more and more transgressive: if there is a space a character feels she/he cannot enter, insist that the 'forbidden' location is occupied. Note the changes to individual and group rhythms. Repeat these until it is possible to switch between (1) neutral, (2) in character and (3) transgressive modes. A transgressive rhythm can be encoded in the playing to signal the disruption of the 'realistic'; to 'speak' against, or to resist the oppressive mechanisms of closure.

Moreover, the choreography of oppressed and transgressive ensemble rhythm/s can be used to re-figure the 'real' through the landscape of the body. Paul Allain's commentary on directing movement for the 1994 revival of *Rutherford and Son* at the National's Cottesloe Theatre, discusses the way in which the actors in rehearsal saw the 'room as consisting of a series of criss-crossing animal tracks, worn by the family members' years of daily patterns' (Allain 1994: 9). Try taking Allain's idea, but re-working it so that the 'daily patterns' of the domestic routines in the spaces which are pointed to but which we do not 'see' are simultaneously played in the 'room' of the father, i.e. upset the boundaries of the fictional space.

Mixing performance registers can also help to demonstrate differences between characters as 'fixed' and accepting of the realistic world in which they are sealed, or as desiring to move 'beyond' its framework. Try, for example, juxtaposing an acting style for Rutherford in which the word, the dominant 'language' in realism, is played against a physical, transgressive register for Mary or Janet, which insists on fragmenting the linguistic.

When exploring the oppressive domestic rituals (Janet's table setting, locking up, removal of the father's boots, Ann's knitting, Mary's sewing, etc.) ensure that the performers also find neutral, in-character, and transgressive registers, so that the domestic may also be represented as a site of refusal.

Working this way, refiguring the 'room' of the father through transgressive ensemble playing, may begin to make the text of the absent present. For instance, the late Mrs Rutherford is hardly referred to but re-presenting the space of the father is a key to refiguring the mother: not as an essentialist reification of the maternal as antidote to the overbearing father, but as a site of material (re)production. Explore, for example, how she comes into view if a verbal reference to her existence is played through Mary as the 'present' body/site of the mother. Or, try exploring links between past/present mothers in an ensemble playing of the dead mother's life in the patriarchal prison and bringing Mary's past life as oppressed working mother into the real domestic space. Play out the transgressive imaging of the mother text, refusing the boundaries of the real through refusing the liminality of the body, the linearity of time, against the patriarchal 'real' in order to make visible that which is repressed.

'Mimicry, and the "true–real"': performance strategies for a feminist mimesis

In her illuminating article 'Mimesis, mimicry, and the "true–real"', Elin Diamond offers a theoretical framing for a feminist praxis where 'mimesis can be retheorized as a site of, and means of, feminist intervention' (Diamond 1989b: 62). Her proposal for a feminist mimesis, or realism, which Diamond describes as 'the modern theater's response to mimesis' (p. 60) is presented through Irigaray's idea of mimesis as mimicry (see Chapter 4, p. 63), and Kristeva's concept of the hysterical body's 'true–real', which Diamond explains:

> suggests that as praxis, the sign-referent model of mimesis can become excessive to itself, spilling into a mimicry that undermines the referent's authority; it also suggests that the interposition of the performer's body signals an interruption of signification itself.
>
> (Diamond 1989b: 62)

It is the locus of the feminist performer that, in Diamond's theoretic, is the key to making a critical intervention in the 'patriarchal modeling'.

Mimicry

Mimesis as mimicry, or 'overmiming', as discussed in Chapter 4, may be useful to the feminist practitioner to interrogate femininity in the 'lost' play projects we have been considering. For example, this might be one way of exploring the oppressed figure of the clinging wife Lily in *Chains*. Stowell's suggestion of taking the dramatic focus away from Charley and 'adjust[ing] one's critical gaze to include Lily and Maggie' so that 'the play is transformed from a tragedy about male paralysis to a comedy of female initiative' (Stowell 1992a: 126), is an interesting one, but problematic unless you can find a way of creating a 'gap' between the performer and the role. By 'overmiming' the role, a performer might find a way of critiquing the text with the body text; of resisting the 'comedy of female initiative' reading that positions Lily as successful in aspiring to and keeping her place in the heteropatriarchal structure of marriage among the lower-middle classes. By overplaying the role, and by drawing attention to its constructedness (e.g. by having the performer read aloud the passive directions for Lily in a way which alienates and refuses them), may, on the other hand, be a way of realising a subversive register. (For more on overplaying, see Love 1995 on her approach to Gwendolyn in Wilde's *The Importance of Being Earnest*.)

'True–Real'

As an illustration of the 'true–real', Diamond takes the example of the prison scene in *Alan's Wife*, where in Scene III, the script includes the instructions: '*Jean's sentences are given as a stage direction of what she is silently to convey, but she does not speak until nearly the end of the Act*' (in Fitzsimmons & Gardner 1991: 23). Diamond explains that:

> Robins and Bell have produced a true–real body: they have given the body axiological (truth-telling) status, but have made it impossible for that body to tell the truth. By wedging a space between the body and the text of the body, Robins and Bell displace the imaginary wholeness of the actor in realism, making her truth provisional, contingent.
>
> (Diamond 1989b: 69)

In the prison scene from *Alan's Wife* you might try exploring this by inviting the performer to play the quietness and stillness of speech and body against a projection of directions and dialogue. As Jean 'scarcely speaks or moves but the play's stage directions *translate* her body "language" into "sentence form"' (*Ibid.*), it introduces a gap between the corporeal/maternal, which comes first, and the 'word', which attempts to transpose the language of the body into words. The projected word might offer a means of heightening its artifice, inadequacy and unreliability, suggesting that the maternal body which speaks first, points to, but also exceeds and refuses the mimetic frame through which it is condemned.

The transgressive ensemble rhythms, 'overmiming', and the 'true–real' are ways that you might try exploring performance registers that point to, even if they cannot represent, that which is not represented. By seeking to undermine the mimetic world as a false truth, then what is 'real' is made 'unreal'. What was suppressed, 'absent', begins to appear, to have 'presence'. We must remember, however, that we only have access to the 'absent' through the 'real'; that in desiring to play 'beyond' the father, we do not necessarily escape the mirror we step through.

RESOURCES

For seminal sources on the 'dangers' of realism try Belsey (1980), Case (1988: Chapter 7, 'Towards a new poetics'), and Dolan (1988: Chapter 5, section, 'The limits of realism'). To examine the 'possibilities of realism' try Stowell (1992a; 1992b), and Schroeder (1996). For a 'feminist actor's approach' to conventional theatre, try Love (1995).

For photographs of Edwardian theatre productions, try library searches for illustrated biographies and autobiographies of performers. Individual histories of theatres often carry production photographs. Try your local theatres for archives of past productions. If you have access to newspaper reviews of productions, these often include sketches of productions, and, in particular, fashion illustrations of women's costumes. Try women's publishing houses for general histories of women's social and cultural lives. Virago Press publications are especially likely to be useful to you, both in terms of modern feminist accounts of the period, and for their recovery of 'lost' texts (fiction and non-fiction) by women.

For further general sources try your local history museums, which may often have artefacts or photographic material that can help with thinking about the past lives and representations of women. Think about oral research and specific communities or groups who might be able to help. For photographs also try your own family albums.

For anthologies of suffrage drama try D. Spender and C. Hayman (eds) *How the Vote Was Won* (London: Methuen, 1985); V. Gardner (ed.) *Sketches From the Actresses' Franchise League* (Nottingham: Nottingham Drama Texts, 1985), and Fitzsimmons and Gardner (1991). On devising suffrage theatre see Clune (1992).

Chapter 7

Activating the feminist script

'A feminist approach to anything means paying attention to women', argues Gayle Austin in the opening to *Feminist Theories for Dramatic Criticism* (1990: 1). 'Paying attention to women' is what, broadly speaking, singles out the work of a number of women writing for contemporary theatre, and whose work might, therefore, according to Austin's definition, be considered 'feminist'. Where the last chapter explored the feminist possibilities and dangers of realism through women's dramatic authorship around the time of the First Women's Liberation Movement, in this chapter I wish to move forward to our modern stage to tackle the issue of how to find a feminist performance register for a feminist play: to look at practical ways of activating the contemporary feminist script.

In the decades following the Second Women's Liberation Movement, feminists writing for and working in theatre have refused to accept the male dominance of mainstream theatrical activity. Consequently, women, individually and collectively, have created a number of plays that have placed women and women's issues centre stage, where parts for women significantly outnumber the roles for men – who may, indeed, be left out altogether. Although there are still relatively few 'plays by women' being published (see the Resources section for suggestions), the growth of feminist theatre studies in the academy during the 1980s has helped to challenge the 'malestream' of canonical dramatic literature, and to move the study of feminist drama and theatre into a less (albeit still) marginal position. In short, it is no longer the case that as young women looking for plays to perform you will automatically have to put on the doublet and hose or pin-striped suit and take the male part.

There is a misguided tendency, however, to think that the feminist play will do the work for you: that, unlike, for example, the performance projects, which require you to make them feminist by playing against form and ideology (as discussed in Chapter 5) and which site the performer as the key critical and political 'text', the feminist script states everything which needs to be said, and the performer's task is merely to act it out. However, a feminist script does not guarantee a feminist performance. As Ellen Donkin and Susan Clement warn, 'a feminist play can slip out from under, even when the director is herself a feminist'. They continue: 'in no case does a production...guarantee a feminist statement. There is the ever-present danger that, without certain checks, we will reflexively reproduce the very gender and racial stereotypes that we ought to be challenging' (Donkin and Clement 1993: 35) .

This chapter aims to explore what those 'checks' might be and to look at the specific difficulties of workshopping and performing the feminist play. The problems of activating the feminist script are located in the discussion of two plays: Charlotte Keatley's *My Mother Said I Never Should* and Caryl Churchill's *Top Girls*, both performed in the 1980s. The two plays share a thematic interest in the representation of the unresolved difficulties that women face in trying to combine motherhood and work, but are radically different in terms of feminist politics, form and style. While *My Mother* is a relatively conservative text, which has acquired a 'radical' reputation, *Top Girls* has suffered a reverse fate as a radical drama that has been misrepresented frequently as a bourgeois–feminist 'success'. Looked at together, these two plays help us to understand the kinds of critical and practical issues that we may find it helpful to consider when approaching feminist drama.

'Paying attention to women': *My Mother Said I Never Should*

My Mother plays with a cast of four women – Doris, her daughter Margaret, granddaughter Jackie and great-granddaughter Rosie – to take a cross-generational look at the lives of these mothers and daughters in the twentieth century. The play is largely set in the domestic sphere, with occasional scenes staged in a 'wasteground' setting in which the four women appear as children. Given the all-female cast, and the dramatisation of women's lives and experiences as mothers and daughters, we can, in a very obvious way, lay claim to the play as 'paying attention to women'. We need, however, to become more thoroughly acquainted with the formal properties and ideological work of Keatley's dramatic text in order to activate it.

One of the reasons why I chose *My Mother* as a working example for this chapter, is my concern for the way in which this play is culturally and pedagogically produced as being at the 'cutting edge' of feminist theatre. Like *Top Girls*, *My Mother* has had mainstream success, was in fact written for 'mainstage spaces' (Keatley 1990a [1988]: Preface), and in recent years has 'made it' on to the Advanced-level syllabus in English secondary schools. The teaching and practice of this play, however, gives serious cause for concern in terms of how students are invited to view the play's feminism, ideological work and dramatic form. When young women discuss their classroom experiences of *My Mother*,[1] they indicate a widespread enthusiasm for the piece that is, understandably, rooted in the opportunity to work on a play that has an all-female cast. Identification lies at the heart of their pleasure response – 'I can see me and my mum in this play. It's just what my mum says', and so on. However, it is misguided to conflate this homogenising response with a claim for the radicalism of the text. The all-female stage picture appears unconventional in relation to the male dominance of our drama and theatre, but this does not necessarily make it a radical play. Similarly, reactions by young women to the form and style of the piece indicate that they regard it as 'highly experimental' and Brechtian, or a mixture of both. They generally identify the experimental quality of the play with the wasteground scenes, and the Brechtian style in the time shifts between scenes. On the other hand, the acting style that these young women generally adopt for the play is that of the psychological, character-based acting method. The practical work that I have seen young women undertaking on this play has been both politically naïve and theatrically uninteresting, largely because the idea that Keatley's feminist script offers an artistic and political challenge has been left unquestioned, and because they have opted for a conventional, 'straight' acting style.

I offer this 'cautionary tale' in order for you to find ways of avoiding these pitfalls, whatever the feminist script your group is working on. First, I would propose that, with the help of your dramaturg, you collectively devise a critical frame from which to think politically and dramatically at the outset of practical work. The aim is not to reduce a play to a single, fixed line of interpretation, but to become aware through critical–practical exploration of the many feminist possibilities that it may yield. Table 1 (Feminisms, forms and registers) offers you a simple critical scheme (though you'll probably want to define your own) for thinking about feminisms in relation to the dramatic text and performance registers. We can explore how this might be useful using *My Mother* as our working example.

To begin: try thinking about feminisms in relation to the dramatic text. You can use parts 1 and 2 of Table 1 to guide you. Keatley claims her own political position as 'socialist and feminist' (Keatley 1990b: 128), and then elsewhere discusses her play as 'female' rather than feminist (Keatley 1997: 75). But what are we to make of Keatley's feminism if we look at how it is encoded at the level of the dramatic? If we work with Table 1 to guide us, then we can see how *My Mother* principally encodes the formal characteristics of a bourgeois–feminist play: it operates predominantly in the realist form, offers strong, character roles, and narrativises women's lives, through naturalistic dialogue. That said, the play's chronological time shifts invite a more deconstructive, materialist approach to structure and narrative organisation; and the de-mystifying, communal playground narratives of how femininity is constructed introduce a stylistic and political shift towards cultural feminism. In brief: the underlying impulse of the text is bourgeois–feminist, while cultural and materialist positions introduce more complex and, in terms of performance, playful and political possibilities.

I am summarising (at the risk of oversimplifying) the kind of critical thinking that is helpful at the outset. I would also advise that rather than pursue your critical thinking in extensive discussion sessions, you think critically through practice. Here are some practical suggestions using the characteristics of the dramatic text in part 2 of Table 1.

• Dramatic form and narrative: try 'cutting and pasting' key moments from the play into chronological biographical narratives. You might try these in monologue style or by organising your group to act out parts in each woman's story. Use this kind of playing to develop your understanding of the extent to which Keatley's play is structurally and ideologically driven by the biographical narrativising of the lives of four individual women, or succeeds in historicising material conditions for women in the twentieth century.
• Characters/Roles/Subjectivity: try creating body sculptures for each of the four women to find out how are they imaged as mothers, daughters, workers, etc. In this way, look to see how far

Table 1 Feminisms, forms and registers

	Bourgeois feminism	Cultural feminism	Materialist feminism
1 Feminisms			
Political aims	to increase opportunities for women in society	to contest the patriarchal organisation of society	to radically transform social, cultural, economic and gender-based systems of oppression
2 Dramatic text			
Form/Narrative	realism; linear and closed; forward-moving; mimetic representation of 'real' time	woman-identified forms of ritual, myth; open, contiguous; collective and cyclical cultural memories	epic; episodic arrangement of scenes: alienation of linear; disjunction of time zones and worlds
Characters/Roles/ Subjectivity	strong roles for women, often represented within domestic and familial spheres	'Woman' as 'Other', as communal, universal, subject; intra-feminine – emphasis on mother/daughter relations	unfixed, state of change and flux, re-configuring and contesting social arrangements; characters marked by difference and diversity of gender, class, sexuality, ethnicity
Dialogue	naturalistic speech forms	resistance to logocentrism	alienation of linguistic sign-system
3 Performance registers			
Acting style Character	psychological 'method' performer and character identification	woman-centred, corporeal 'Woman' as performer	'not…but' demonstration non-identification of performer and role; multiple role playing
Verbal and non-verbal sign-systems	dominance of verbal sign-system	foregrounding of non-verbal, 'speaking' body	historicisation of body and word

Keatley represents orthodox models of mothering, or how far she challenges conservative representations of maternity/femininity through unorthodox imaging (e.g. of single parenting). Or, try working in pairs, taking one character each and improvise sequences in which you switch between the adult and the child of your characters, sometimes playing as two adult women, as adult and child, or as two children. Keep switching until you find movements and key lines for each. Try this to develop a sense of how far subjectivity is represented as stable or in flux; to explore how far the child/adult technique of playing constitutes a way of interrogating subjectivity.

• Dialogue: try looking at scenes to see how dominant the verbal text is. Explore Keatley's own claim to a style of 'visual theatre', which prioritises the image over the word (Keatley 1990b: 133). Try acting out scenes to develop a sense of how far you feel Keatley offers the performer a way into a non-verbal, physical performance register, or is more concerned with a word-based text, shaped through the conventional realist mode of 'naturalistic', turn-taking sequences of dialogue. Try miming a scene and discover how far you feel you 'author' gesture and movement as the practitioner, or how far you feel Keatley 'directs' you towards this through her script. Or, try finding key words and key lines to direct the rhythms of speech in order to explore the heightened verbal language which, Keatley argues, is also characteristic of her 'visual theatre'. Are there key words for different characters? Try to feel how far Keatley pushes speech towards a heightened verbal language, or how far you feel encouraged into 'realistic' registers.

Working along these critical and practical lines you are also discovering more about the possible performance registers (Table 1, part 3) both suggested by the script, and by yourselves as practitioners coming to the script. While on the one hand analysis reveals the relative conservatism (formally and politically) of *My Mother*, this does not mean, on the other, that you have to endorse the conservatism in your workshop practice. Rather than a 'straight', psychological acting style in line with the dominant realist style of the play (see Table 1, part 3), in which feminism may well 'slip out from under', you can activate those registers that will heighten moments of radicalism in the text, or more thoroughly radicalise the text in performance.

For example: Act I, sc. vi is a sentimentalised, mother-gives-baby-away scene, as Jackie hands over her baby daughter Rosie to her mother Margaret to look after. If you wanted to activate this scene through a woman-centred, cultural–feminist performance register, then you might want to re-work it through a corporeally chore-ographed visual, wordless scene that foregrounds the discourse of the maternal body. Working around key mother and child objects (not necessarily those used in the script, but found by participants and brought in to workshop) would be one way to try this. Gradually, key lines might be added to key choreographed images, brought, finally, into the text-based scene.

Alternatively, the same scene could be activated through a materi-alist–feminist register that might aim for a 'not but' style of Brechtian-inflected materialist playing to raise more extensive ques-tions about the social conditions of mothering. For example, hints of Brechtian techniques in this scene could be exploited to avoid over-sentimentalisation and to heighten the social critique. You could try re-telling the scene as a reported past event. The Brechtian sheet-as-baby device could be used throughout the scene (rather than at the end of it) to diffuse the emotional intensity and re-direct it towards a political awareness of reproductive 'choice' for women. Try announcing titles for the scene, or finding images or text to project behind the playing that make you aware of the material conditions of reproduction in a capitalist society, and so on.

Remember that ultimately these don't have to be 'either/ors' – that the pleasures of feminist theatre practice are often to be found in those critical, political and creative moments that mix feminisms, forms and registers.

Bourgeois–feminist project or radical critique?: *Top Girls*

Top Girls is Caryl Churchill's internationally acclaimed critique of the Thatcherite 'Superwoman'. Opening with a transhistorical dinner scene that brings together 'great' women from fiction, art, history and legend to celebrate top girl Marlene's 'success', the plays moves to the 'present' in an employment agency for women (of which Marlene is now the 'boss'), and chronologically backwards to a year earlier, to stage a confrontation scene between Marlene and her working-class sister, Joyce, who has care of Marlene's biological daughter, Angie.

If the danger of Keatley's script is that what is essentially a bourgeois–feminist play is culturally and pedagogically produced as
materialist feminism, then the risk in activating Churchill's *Top Girls*
is that a materialist–feminist script may be reduced to a
bourgeois–feminist hymn in praise of the 'top girl' ethos. (This was
how some spectators, particularly American spectators, received the
first professional productions of *Top Girls* (see Reinelt, 1994, note 28:
221–2).

In her account of directing *Top Girls* , Julie Thompson Burk refers
to the ways in which *Top Girls* may read differently according to
perspective:

> Read from the point of view of the dominant ideology of
> Western culture, *Top Girls* is a play about a successful if some-
> what heartless career woman, Marlene, and her bitter
> working-class sister Joyce. Read from the perspective of this
> materialist–feminist, however, the play shifts its focus to the sacri-
> fices Marlene has had to make to achieve success and the choices
> women like Marlene and her sister, Joyce, don't have in contem-
> porary society.
>
> (Burk 1993: 67)

Burk explains that her line of interpretation was a 'problematizing of
Marlene's success' (p. 72), and that she used Nancy Hartsock's *Money,
Sex, and Power*, more specifically Hartsock's 'contention that class
society is the means by which women participate in their own
oppression' (Burk 1993: 67) to theoretically frame her directing of
Churchill's play (which you may also find a useful departure point).
Here, however, I propose a brief return to Table 1, again to establish
the premise that understanding the textual apparatus of the text can
help us in 'reading' the play's feminism, and that if we read from the
'dominant ideology of Western culture', we are actually reading
against what is in the text.

A dramatic analysis of narrative, character and dialogue in *Top
Girls* reveals the play's dominant feminist dynamic as
materialist–feminist. Narrative is ruptured by a non-linear sequencing
of scenes from the opening transhistorical dinner scene, through the
present-day office scenes of the 'top girls' agency, to the confrontation
between the sisters Marlene and Joyce. Techniques of overlapping
dialogue heighten the artifice of 'naturalistic' speech. Past and present
histories are used to critique and to contest the class- and gender-

based oppression of women. Deconstructive and distancing strategies, such as the doubling or tripling of parts, refuse the 'top girl' success story; both formally and ideologically the play problematises rather than accepts the bourgeois–feminist position embodied in Marlene (the one character who significantly is not 'unfixed' through multiple role-playing).

Critical analysis can establish the encoding of a materialist–feminist position in the dramatic text – the difficulty is how we activate it in performance and invite people to *see* it (although remember that ultimately, you can only invite – you can't make people see what they don't want to see). As we already have the Keatley example to demonstrate how we can extend critical analysis into practical work-shopping, I propose to use *Top Girls* to look in more detail at practical suggestions for activating the script through a materialist–feminist performance register: of trying to ensure that the radicalism of the text does not slip away from us in practice.

Alienating gender and class

The materialist–feminist dynamic of *Top Girls* is centrally located in its critique of bourgeois–feminist values. Here are some proposals for activating a materialist–feminist critique of bourgeois feminism through workshop practice.

Re-presenting superwoman

To interrogate the figure of Marlene as successful career woman, your group could collect images or descriptions of career women to work into a montage to mount in your workshop space. For example, look for images in magazines, newspapers, or on the covers of novels. Pick out captions from newspaper articles that describe successful career women. To be effective, the montage needs to be as full as possible. Try enlarging some images and captions that you feel are dominant or central to the representation of the 'Superwoman' figure, so that they impact on your working space.

Next, everyone needs to respond to the montage. Discuss how far this represents the lives of women in the group, or those of their female friends, colleagues and relatives. Think about what or who is left out, and then undertake another search for the 'missing' images, and insert these (if they can be found) into the collage in order to fragment the 'Superwoman' ethos.

Alternatively, you could try collaging the top-girl images into a 'missing' image or shape. Use the images of career women, for example, to fill the shape of a mother-with-pram outline or a silhouette of Madonna-with-child (for examples of this kind of collage work see Davis and Goodall 1987: 294).

Your group could be invited to look at how the overlaid or reshaped collage changes. How is difference inserted into the imaging? What does this say about how women are represented. Where are *you* in the montage? In short, what does the 'Superwoman' make invisible: in the representation of 'top girls' does motherhood become invisible (note that girls implies an infantalisation, arrested development), or is motherhood represented as the privilege of top-earning women, which makes the working-class mother invisible?

Try using the 'Superwoman' images as a visual aid or point of reference for developing movement and gestural patterns for the 'top girl' figures. Include both the top girls of the dinner scene and the agency women. Try and choreograph gestures that might eventually be encoded or overlaid in an ensemble playing of the top girl figure – a language of oppression performed through a physical register.

Looking back again at the montage, focus on the 'missing' images and use these to create and choreograph oppositional movement patterns to the top girls choreography. Each woman should have a set of five 'top girl' gestures and five gestures that belong to the 'invisible', oppressed or repressed mother-figure. Each woman could be encouraged to memorise her sets of empowered and disempowered gestures. Try these out in oppositional pairs. Both participants should be allowed to swap between sequences so that they experience the physical, gestural encoding of both representations.

Mistress and servant

When Monstrous Regiment rehearsed for their production of Wendy Kesselman's *My Sister in this House*, based on the case of the Papin sisters, two live-in servants who murdered their mistress and her daughter, they created a ritual that was played out daily throughout the rehearsal period. The two actresses playing the mistress and daughter sat down to coffee, while the actresses playing the servant sisters had to clean the rehearsal room (see Hanna 1991: lxvii) Try developing your own mistress-and-servant rituals. For example, while Nell and Win take coffee, Joyce scrubs the floor. Or stage an office scene in which Joyce is constantly cleaning while Marlene is engaged in office work. This may help you to explore the class and gender issues that resonate in Joyce's insistence that she and Marlene cannot be friends.

Joyce is a key figure in the critique of Marlene's success. To describe her as 'bitter' (Burk 1993: 67) tends to personalise rather than politicise her, and overlooks the possibility of activating Joyce's discourse as one of working-class anger, pride and resistance. To find a political voice for working-class women, rather than a personal, 'bitter' voice of Joyce as an individual woman, try creating a monologue for Joyce (à la Sarah Daniels), using key lines that reflect on her life, class and politics. You could try delivering this punctuated by key top-girl lines ('poor working girl', 'she's not going to make it', 'there's not a lot of room upward'), which demonstrate a class hierarchy, but which leave Joyce with the dominant linguistic space. You might also try playing monologues you devise for Joyce with extracts from other working-class voices (from other feminist plays, perhaps, or historical sources).

Alternatively, try inserting feminist theorisations of class oppression into top girl scenes. You might, for example, try this using extracts from the Hartsock text that Burk used. Or try out this idea by inserting the Black voice of American feminist–activist, bell hooks, to create a Brechtian style of commentary to critique the bourgeois feminism of the top girl ethos. To give an example:

hooks:	It is evident that large numbers of individual white women (especially those from middle-class backgrounds) have made economic strides in the wake of feminist movement support of careerism…
Nell:	I've a lady here thinks she can sell.
Win:	Taking her on?
hooks:	and affirmative action programs in many professions.
Nell:	She's had some jobs.
Win:	Services?
hooks:	However, the masses of women are as poor as ever, or poorer.
Nell:	No, quite heavy stuff, electric.
Win:	Tough bird like us.
hooks:	To the bourgeois 'feminist,' the million dollar salary granted newscaster Barbara Walters represents a victory for women.
Nell:	We could do with a few more here.

Win:	There's nothing going here.
hooks:	To working class women who make less than the minimum wage…
Nell:	No but I always want the tough ones when I see them…
hooks:	…and receive few if any benefits…
Nell:	Hang onto them.
hooks:	it means continued class exploitation.
Win:	I think we are plenty.

(Churchill 1990: 102; hooks 1984: 59)

Remember: if you are working as an all-white group of women, then be sensitive to the racial issue of a white woman speaking and colonising the Black voice. A collage that heightens race as well as class as a factor in working and mothering images might help.

Top and bottom texts

Reinelt gives an example from Churchill's play *Mad Forest* (1990), a response to the political and revolutionary upheavals in Romania, of what she describes as a 'top and bottom' text. A young Romanian woman goes to a doctor seeking an abortion:

> They speak a 'politically correct' top text, in which he tells her to get married and that there is no abortion in Romania, while the bottom text shows the exchange of money and agreement about the procedure.
>
> (Reinelt 1994: 103)

The top and bottom texts idea can be applied to practical explorations where you might want to bring out conflicts in meaning: between what is being said, and what is *really* being said, or implied. Such points of conflict can heighten your awareness of class boundaries and confrontation.

For example, you could try developing a top and a bottom text for the Marlene and Angie encounter in Marlene's office (Act II, sc. iii), which makes visible the gap between their lives. While Marlene politely verbalises her 'pleasure' at Angie's unexpected arrival, try creating a visual 'text' that 'speaks' her displeasure. Heightened body language can be one way of communicating this, but you might also try working with props or an absence of them. When Marlene invites Angie to sit down, for example, make sure there is no chair for her to sit on. When Marlene agrees to the arrangements for Angie to stay overnight, have her busily consult train or bus time-tables to see how quickly she might actually be able to arrange her departure.

You can also try using the top and bottom text idea for making the lack of desire/s, which are invisible or repressed in the top girl adoption of oppressive capitalist and patriarchal systems, visible. Find objects that can be used to stand in for the repressed desire – a rose for Win perhaps, or an engagement ring for Jeanine. As characters speak their top text, allow them to indulge in fetishistic play with the object that speaks their absent desire. In Jeanine's interview, allowing us to see her wearing and drawing attention to the ring she talks about not wearing, might allow us to see the dichotomy between marriage and career.

'Death-space'

In the closure of *Fen*, Churchill's exploration of gender and class exploitation in the East Anglian fen community, Val, the central protagonist is 'murdered' by her lover, and the episodic, realistic scenes that constitute the dramatic form up until that moment are displaced by a surreal landscape in which figures from the community are given a resistant voice to 'speak' their pain and the opportunities denied to them. Diamond discusses this moment in *Fen* as Churchill's re-figuring of female bodies in a 'death-space', and stresses the ability of this space to make visible the invisible; the repressed 'stories' of women's bodies that are 'silenced' in the 'visible world' (Diamond 1989c: 273).

Try out the idea of a 'death-space' for *Top Girls*. Try devising a 'death-space' that attempts to make visible the invisible lives of the working-class women we see oppressed in the play. What are the desires and stories that might be 'ghosted' into this space and be made 'visible'? How might a 'death-space' for the figures of Joyce and Angie enable them to be 'seen' or heard differently?

One final suggestion here: try mixing a 'death-space' with the 'real'. To give an example: try choreographing a 'death-space' using the figures from the dinner scene to haunt the domestic encounter between Marlene and Joyce. We developed this idea in a student production of *Top Girls* at Loughborough University (Summer 1991), so that while the sisters occupied a lit area of the set, the figures from the 'past' were figures in shadow – still, silent onlookers, spectators who watched and listened to their oppression being played out again in the present (also the future). As the confrontation between the sisters reached its final impasse, a physical echoing of the climax to the dinner scene (the moment when the women's bodies are vomiting, spewing, and playing out the registers of pain, violence and anguish of their male-dominated lives), was choreographed to Angie's final line, 'Frightening'. The 'death-space' did not, in this instance, articulate repressed desires, but it did make visible the never-ending cycle of inter- and intra-sexual oppression.

Narrative

Workshopping narrative organisation of the dramatic text helps you to understand the interrogative properties of the dramatic text: to heighten your awareness through practice of the play's formal and ideological resistance to closure.

Gestic playing

Try out a gestic exploration of narrative by working out a *Gestus* (either taken from the script, or perhaps, by improvising your own), which summarises the play overall, each act, and each scene. Churchill's titles for the three-act structure, which is how the play is set out in later editions (see Churchill 1990), can help you with this: Act I, the dinner, Act II, Angie's story and Act III, the year before. (Originally the play was performed with only one interval and the drama was presented in two acts, as in the 1982 or 1984 editions.) You might choose to see the waitress serving the other women as a key *Gestus* for Act I; Angie in her ill-fitting dress, which reflects her inability to fit in to Marlene's life and world, might be seen as a gestic representation of Act II (see Reinelt 1994: 91–2); and Marlene's inappropriate present buying, which demonstrates the middle- and working-class economic and cultural clashes, might be explored as the social *Gestus* for Act III. The waiting on women may emerge as a key *Gestus* for the play overall. Remember, however, that there is no right and no wrong about this. Instead, all women in the group should be encouraged to represent the scenes gestically to see how different responses affect and help to arrive at a shared understanding of narrative and ideology.

Re-positioning scenes

Churchill invites us to choose whether to present *Top Girls* as a two-
or three-act drama (Churchill 1990: 54). You could experiment
further with organisational structure by re-positioning scenes, or
extracts from scenes, to heighten your sense of the distancing and
politicising techniques that inform Churchill's writing. For example,
you could underline the oppressive intra-sexual dynamic of the interview scenes by a multiple playing of the Marlene and Jeanine, Win
and Louise, and Nell and Shona scenes. Try not to let the anxiety or
threat of incoherence be off-putting. Organising a polyphony of
oppressive encounters raises energy levels that may (1) intensify your
sense of intra-sexual oppression and (2) heighten your sense of
urgency for feminist agency to change this.

Alternatively, you could try mixing interview scenes or Marlene
and her 'fellow' top girl scenes into the Kit and Angie scene (Act II,
sc. ii) to increase awareness of how 'frightening' female participation
in and acceptance of Western capitalism is to the younger generation
of teenage women.

Character

Churchill's convention of doubling or tripling characters is a direct
invitation to a 'not...but' style of materialist–feminist playing that
resists the dangers of the Method-based acting technique and the
process of performer/character identification. By showing the gap
between performer and role, you open up the possibilities of demonstrating resistance rather than acceptance of oppressive structures.
Workshopping that helps to explore this 'gap' might include, for
example, stepping out of role and commenting on your character's
actions as you play them, using other members of your group as an
audience, or using Brechtian reporting techniques to distance yourself from the dialogue.

Character narratives

Playing the characters in the restaurant scene is generally an experience that creates high energy levels among performers who need to
concentrate hard on the overlapping dialogue techniques that
generate much of the energy and underpin the varying levels of
emotional intensity that shape the act. For work on characters in this

scene, you could use the character narratives in the edition of *Top Girls* designed for the schools and overseas reader (Churchill: 1991). Present these individual narratives as a materialist–feminist critique, by, for example, narrating them through a collective ensemble playing that physically and linguistically alienates systems of gender and class oppression.

Alternatively, try the sources that Churchill used for the writing of *Top Girls* for further character and narrative work (see the Resources section). For example, try Pat Barr's *A Curious Life for a Lady*, which Churchill used for her research into Isabella Bird as a devising source (Barr: 1970). Extract one or two incidents from Barr's biographical narrative and re-present these gestically to highlight a gender issue. You can always 'ghost' this kind of devising into a playing out of a *Top Girls* scene. Try re-presenting one of Isabella's travel episodes and 'ghosting' this against Angie's arrival in London when she explains how she has travelled down to see her 'aunt' (Act II sc. iii).

'Not but' character and costume play

In her theorisation of Churchill's work, which draws on French feminist theory and Brechtian theory, Elin Diamond proposes Churchill's 'feminist project' as one in which there is 'no "writing the body"', but rather a foregrounding of the apparatus that makes the writing impossible' (Diamond 1989c: 262). Diamond describes the costumes for the characters in the *Top Girls* dinner scene as 'elaborate historical text[s]' that situate the women in 'Western representation' while their 'words…refer to need, violence, loss, and pain, to a body unable to signify within those texts' (Diamond 1989c: 266).

Try exploring ways in which the 'apparatus' of costuming can help foreground the oppressive systems of gender representation. Look for costume props that can help find a 'not but' style of playing for each character: a register that states 'this represents me, but is not really me'. You could add an object prop to a clothing prop and women could improvise their own physical sequences. This could be organised as a ritual, with performers being invited to set their objects in the space, to work through their own improvised sequences, and helped to find a (ritualised) way of being left in the space. Working and re-working a ritualised sequence may help a performer to find a physical text of remembered gestures that can be introduced into the acting out of a scene.

You can also try costume-prop work to explore gender exploitation in the agency scenes to look at gender 'distortions' of the body. In the process of transforming a spectator into actor in his forum theatre, Boal explains how a first stage of work is designed to look at the 'social distortions' of the body (Boal 1979: 126). He explains:

> There is a great number of exercises designed with the objective of making each person aware of his (*sic*) own body, of his (*sic*) bodily possibilities, and of deformations suffered because of the type of work he (*sic*) performs. That is, it is necessary for each one to feel the 'muscular alienation' imposed on his body by work.
>
> (Boal 1979:127)

You can take Boal's idea to explore the 'muscular alienation' of the secretary's body hunched over a typewriter or wordprocesser. Try using the follow-my-leader exercise cited in Chapter 3 (p. 49). To look at the gender as well as 'social distortions', add in costume props to look at how outfits of femininity in the workplace also 'deform' the body. Try, for example, working with shoulder pads, tight-fitting skirts that restrict movement, or try walking and working in high-heeled shoes.

Roles for men?

A group that has a male and female constituency, with women in the majority and men in the minority, is often argued by student groups as a reason for not tackling plays like *Top Girls* or *My Mother*, which have women-only casts. This a view that I have heard argued by both male and female students. It was a departure point for the student production I cited earlier, which created a very difficult dynamic (although by no means, not the only one) in the production process. This, I would argue, is a dangerous view, because if adhered to, then it effectively keeps women's work off-stage, and merely reinforces the unequal *status quo*.

Rather than see such a project as at worst, impossible, or, at best, resolved by having the men involved in backstage activities, the men might be invited to try cross-gender casting (see also sections on cross-gendered play in Chapters 4 and 5). When teaching during the 1980s, I saw some very interesting student workshopping of *Top Girls* that came out of cross-gender casting. Men tend to be very apprehensive about the idea of playing women's roles, contrary to the way in which women have always found themselves having to take the 'male part', and have generally accepted this as a 'norm'. While I would argue that cross-gender casting that plays for laughs and is ideologically damaging in its ridiculing and belittling of women is to be discouraged, getting men to play women 'straight' can help to demonstrate gender, power and class struggles. An office scene played between two men can immediately demonstrate the 'gap' between performer and role, and the ideological work that this 'gap' reveals, because the actor has to find ways of putting on the female habitus of either the empowered 'top girl' or disempowered client.

Instructing an actor to play a female role 'straight' is a way of helping him to 'suspend' the power he has by being male, and to engage in the inequalities of gender-based oppression. An actor who, after much persuading, took on the role of the waitress in the dinner scene in the student production, for example, did not attempt to conceal his own body, but allowed it to be seen and encoded with signs of oppressed femininity (e.g. white, frilled apron). The stylistic register for the actor's performance was different to that of the women participating in the dinner scene. As a silent, stylised slow-motion performance juxtaposed with the energies of the dining women, it ritualised the activity of waiting at table into a political statement regarding female servitude.

In mixed groups, this kind of cross-gender experiment can help men to participate in making theatre feminist without the danger, as I warned in Chapter 2, of disempowering women. Moreover, Churchill's own cross-gender or cross-race casting in other plays (*Cloud Nine*, for example), suggests that this is a way of exploring her theatre that is in-keeping with the dramatist's own ludic vision of role playing.

To summarise: whatever the script you are working on – whether canonical or feminist – always research your dramatic text to be certain of how it operates, both formally and ideologically. Once you have a firm critical–practical understanding of what is 'in' a text then you can decide how to activate it. Remember: not all scripts referred to as feminist necessarily advocate a position you wish to endorse. What all of the chapters in Part II of this book have shown is a recourse to a materialist–feminist practice in the interests of finding transgressive, gender- and class-aware registers of playing. Many of the materialist–feminist suggestions raised here will also be useful to bring to proposals outlined in Part III, as we move to consider a feminist practice in which you are looking to create your own texts.

RESOURCES

The 'Plays By Women' series published by Methuen is a useful way to begin to find your way around feminist playwriting for the modern stage. There are currently ten volumes in the series, and the editorial and authorial introductions to the volumes and to individual play scripts offer contextualising information that often includes observations on the writing and rehearsal processes. Also useful are the anthologies of women's plays published by Aurora Metro, which include volumes on Black and Asian women dramatists and on European plays by women. For collections of plays by contemporary American women playwrights try Applause Theatre Books, who produce a number of woman-authored anthologies. Nick Hern Books (UK) has a commitment to new playwriting (by women and men), and is therefore a good starting place for researching recent work. A few women playwrights have managed to have their work anthologised. Volumes you might try sampling from include: Caryl Churchill (Methuen and Nick Hern); Sarah Daniels (Methuen); Louise Page (Methuen); Sharman Macdonald (Methuen) Christina Reid (Methuen), and Timberlake Wertenbaker (Faber).

For contextualising studies that will help you to find your way around the field of women's playwriting try Aston (1995a), Case (1988), or Goodman (1993).

Methuen have published student editions of both *My Mother* and *Top Girls*. While the commentaries and notes in these editions tend to be quite basic and explanatory in approach, they are useful for workshopping purposes: to resource devising work away from the text on narrative, character, and dialogue, etc. Churchill often reveals sources that have influenced her writing of a play and these can again be useful materials to activate in the workshop. Some basic workshopping suggestions for *Top Girls* can be found in Michaels and Sawyer (1993), and on directing *Top Girls* see Burk (1993).

Part III

Gender and devising projects

Working without a theatre script is both an exciting challenge and a frightening way to practise theatre. There is a journey ahead that is unknown, dangerous, full of risk, fear, exhilaration, energy, creativity and much more. When it is a woman who finds the script, through her own body and in her own words, she has first to find the body, the words and the confidence to speak out; to be seen and to be heard (see Chapter 3). When we have scripts, there are characters and words given to us, and we can hide behind them if we need to. Creating our own texts and sharing them through performance is a huge and exciting task, and an enormous challenge for women.

At some point, however daunting at the outset, this is a journey you will want to make. Where you go, what you do, and who and what you see, and, ultimately, invite others to see and to share, will depend on where you have come from, and where you would like to travel to: creatively, politically, emotionally, personally. The map I am offering in the remaining chapters uses case study examples of specific devising projects to chart further exercises and practical ideas to pack into your 'kit bag' as you set off on your own creative journeys; find your own routes to travel.

Chapter 8

Creating texts

Creating texts through the agency and creativity of the performer is what characterises devising work. We noted at the outset of this study that the process of devising is especially important to women who are marginalised by dominant culture and theatre and therefore have most to gain from 'authoring' their own scripts. In Part II, we touched on a number of ways in which women can use devising techniques in relation to scripted work – for example, in order to challenge the authority of a canonical script, or to activate a feminist position within a dominant cultural form such as realism. Here, in Part III, however, I concentrate on non-scripted work: with feminist devising projects in which women create their own scripts.

In the opening section of this chapter, I present physical ways of 'writing'; of starting to generate fragments of text. These fragments may remain as workshopped fragments, or, alternatively, may become the starting point for a devised project.

However, starting from 'zero' to create your own scripts can be an exceptionally daunting proposition: how do you decide on a feminist subject, agree to shape it and ultimately to perform it? In the second part of this chapter, therefore, I look at the idea of adapting a non-theatre text, a short story, for feminist performance. Working from a non-theatre, word-based source gives you a 'hook to hang things on' – particularly if you feel the need for an experience-building exercise to give you the confidence and skill to start scripting original material on your own.

Finally, to illustrate the adaptation process, I conclude with a brief case study of a student adaptation of Angela Carter's *The Bloody Chamber*. I realise that in detailing specific examples of feminist devising in the academy, as I do in this and the subsequent two chapters, I refer to creative work that usually has no 'life' or 'authority' beyond the moment of its showing (for more on this point see Harris 1994). The devised work is 'resurrected' here in another 'life' (print) form as a further means of trying to 'hand on' ideas for future feminist practice.

Body-writing

In the text-generating exercises that follow, I am thinking specifically of the devising context in which a group of performers are to play a central role in creating the text – possibly with the dramaturg/s taking overall responsibility for scripting. However, these exercises are also useful to writers, coming to or working in groups, who are willing to share script development with devising-performers. However, remember the advice in Chapter 2 about being clear about what is expected of whom (see p. 34), in order to avoid difficulties and tensions.

Moreover, before your group embarks on the following kinds of body-writing exercises, be sure to follow the advice in Chapter 3 and begin by giving yourselves the time and space to get in touch with your 'physical' selves. None of the body-writing suggestions offered here will work if bodies are still 'locked' into heads. Remember: your vocal warm-ups (see p. 52) can be especially useful for checking to see whether participants are relaxed and 'speaking' from the stomach/pelvic area, or are still tense and have voices locked away in the upper chest area. Never be afraid to spend as much time as the group needs on getting physically in touch with themselves. You may find, for example, that whole sessions are devoted to this at the outset of a project, and even as your group begins to body-think and body-write more quickly and you spend less time on warm-ups and more time on creating your material, never be tempted to start 'cold'.

Themed warm-ups

You may wish to organise a warm-up that takes you into a particular feminist theme or issue your group plans to work on.

To give a very simple example, a workshop on envy might begin with a general physical and vocal warming-up. One woman is then given an object, which she tries to keep to herself, but the rest of the group try to take away from her. Whoever has the coveted object is 'it' and chased by the group (a reverse game of tag where one person chases the group). [1] If energy levels are high (especially likely if you have a good number of women in your group who are chasing, and the person carrying the object is caught very quickly so that there's a rapid changing over of roles), you can push this into improvising text. Try never to think about the words. Just let them come up through the physical playing. It is also helpful if your dramaturg or a member of the group writes down the words. Remember that any of your improvised 'text' can be discarded, or, you can elect to keep any one word, or words, or lines of dialogue. Trust the group's instinct.

You may pre-plan a themed session, as in the envy example, or you may find that a warm-up begins spontaneously to move in a particular direction, in which case trust the creative flow of your group and go with it. Always be prepared to go with the physical dynamic, emotional patterns and energies of your group. There are no rules about how this happens, except that you need always to be thinking with your bodies and not with your heads. Thinking with heads will only force or rather 'block' your words.

Sticks and words

Try the stick exercise (p. 50) and when energy levels are high and co-ordination is good within your group, try adding in sounds. Use whatever rhythm the group is in to create the sound. Move from sounds into words. You can experiment with free association – words that are suggested by the rhythm. Or you may organise your dramaturg to feed key words to the group (perhaps related to a particular issue or topic you are thinking of working on), who in turn come up with any word associated with the key word, but always keeping with the rhythmic body flow of the stick work. The words are offered when a participant is in the act of throwing a stick.

Music into words

Your group could select a piece of music to work with. Try to find pieces that provide a stimulus for movement, but do not suggest a story that is already known. For example, avoid the theme music to a film if known to your group because it will be hard to move away from the suggestion of the cinematic narrative. Your dramaturg or group could research pieces appropriate to the mood or theme you wish to work in/on, and can freely associate with. Work on impro-vised movement to your music for as long as you need to (probably over several sessions), and participants could be invited to extract a brief series of physical 'moments' from their movement sequence –

perhaps up to six 'moments'. Each participant could freeze-frame their six 'moments'. For each of these 'moments', women watching the freeze-frames could propose a word or line to accompany the image. Your dramaturg can make a note of these. Ultimately, you may wish to select those images and words you wish to keep and to work from. Remember you can always play with putting a 'moment' against a different word in your record to see what happens. You can also experiment collectively with a simultaneous choreographed play of images and words.

'Fabricating' words

Each participant could bring a different piece of fabric to the group. The pieces should be concealed. Each woman in turn produces her piece of fabric for the group while the others have their eyes closed. The piece of fabric should be placed in the centre of the group and everyone allowed to explore it through touch and smell. Group members should be invited to associate with the material, suggesting words that connect with the texture, the feel, the smell of the fabric, and so on. Again, you may wish to have a record of the words that surface in response to different fabrics. The group are allowed to see the fabric after the word-association playing is over.

Your group may wish to take this further into filling a designated space with the different fabrics. Each woman places her fabric in the space. When all the fabrics are laid out, any woman can make adjustments to the arrangement of the material until the whole group is satisfied with the visual display. Think about the different colours and textures you have; the contrasts, clashes, brightness, depth and surface of the display. Each woman can then place herself somewhere in the arrangement. She may wish to bury herself in a piece of cloth, or feel a piece of fabric against her face. Put words into the fabric frame – possibly words from the previous work, or perhaps new words, new associations. If this work is going forward into project work, arrange to photograph your fabric setting, as well as keeping a record of your words.

You can experiment in this kind of way with different sorts of materials depending on the kind of project you have in mind. You could try this exercise with different types and pieces of wood for example, or different pebbles and stones. If you work with stones – try creating a 'magic ring' of stones to step in and out of. See how you feel inside and outside of the circle, and whether there are stories which begin to emerge. Whatever you choose to work with, always introduce the kind of trigger you are proposing at the outset to ensure that the group is comfortable with what they are to touch unseen. If this is not properly introduced, then participants may feel anxious and 'blocked'.

'Elemental' objects

We have strong emotional and mythical attachments to the elements: earth, fire, water, air. Try working with these as stimuli: a bowl of water or earth, a candle for fire, or a hand-held fan to create a flow of air. Concentrate on just one element at a time. With water, for example, each woman could be invited to dip her hand into the bowl, allowing the water to trickle through her fingers to see which emotions, memories or stories come to the surface. Or, participants could be asked to focus on the flame of a lighted candle to see what memories are evoked.

Another exercise you can try is to work with an element to see if there are any ancient, mythical or fairy stories triggered, from childhood memories perhaps. For example, when I focused on a flame my first story that I came up with was the children's rhyme: 'Ladybird, Ladybird fly away home/ Your house is on fire/ Your children are gone'. My association is not an event, but an emotional reaction: fear for the safety of my own children, especially if I am away from them.

See if there are any shared stories in the group. This does not necessarily mean that women remember the same story, but there may be narrative similarities. You can develop this further into personal memories of why the story is significant in your memory: a special book you remember being read to you; an association with a special event in your life; a painful or happy memory, etc. Make a note of all of these as a record to carry forward.

For example, try choreographing a group movement as a response to a particular fairy story, while allowing an individual participant to speak her own memory of an event or an emotion she associates with that story. You can play with finding a group movement and possibly adding in sound as a kind of chorus to the woman who offers her own words, her own narration over the top of this.

Everyday objects

In contrast to 'elemental' objects, working with objects we use everyday can also be a productive way of body-writing. For example, try finding different kinds of drinking vessels to work with – coffee mugs, tea cups, wine glasses, beer glasses and so on. Play with these and tell a story you associate with whichever type of cup you are working with. You can go on to experiment with creating a group sound text to accompany the woman who has the narrative voice in a given moment.

If you are working with everyday objects in a particular stage setting, it can be useful to try this kind of exercise to find out what a specific chair, table or cup means to a particular performer/character. Remember everyday objects on the stage assume greater significance, and it is important for performers to explore their 'larger-than-life-everydayness' as well as working with objects which have symbolic, highly significant properties.

You can also work on everyday objects that you feel are particularly gender specific. Try organising an installation of such objects, and improvising en-gendered narratives, feelings, sounds.

Colours

Like the music exercise suggested earlier, working with colours is a way of working from an abstract register through to a concrete, word-based mode. A few suggestions for generating words through colour are as follows:

- Lying down, with eyes closed and bodies relaxed, think of a memory and give it a colour. Try vocalising the colour you have given your memory, allowing the emotion of the memory to resonate in the colour.
- Lying down, eyes closed, and, breathing deeply, focus on a colour and let the colour out through sound. You can experiment with your group working on the same colour or an orchestra of different colours. Appoint one woman to conduct your orchestra of colours by touching each woman at different moments to cue her in and out of the colour-sound text. You can keep working on this moving from sounds into words.

- Or, you can play this again by inviting each woman to focus (1) on the colour she sees herself, and (2) the colour she'd like to be, and switching between the two, working in sounds and words.
- Try playing with colours physically asking women to move with the colour in which they see themselves and with the colour they would like to be. See what happens to movements in different colours. If there are words that come with the movements, then add these in. Or, just speak the name of the colour in the movement.

Imaging women

Visual materials (photographs, advertisements, etc.) that offer different representations of women are useful for generating images and narratives. Your dramaturg could research images appropriate to a project you have in mind. Half of your group could stage these as freeze-frames, while the other half could look at the frames and give the women (and men) in them names, words and lines. Find out what the relationships, stories and attitudes between particular figures are. Select two figures to focus on, and have two women who are viewing the 'photograph' to feed lines to each of the two figures. Suggest that your dramaturg keep a note of any of the text generated that the group might feel it would be useful to develop, and continue working in more figures and more narratives.

Body sentences

Try feeding lines to participants, but breaking the line so that they only have half of it and have to complete the sentence physically.

Alternatively, start with a physical gesture that begins with one woman and is completed by words from another. You can play with this in a specific topic or issue-related context, or experiment with free improvisations and associations to see what happens.

You can continue playing by building a string of body–word sequences: Woman A gestures to B, who responds in words carried on using gestures by C, moved back into words by D, and so on. Group members should have the opportunity to play with both words and gestures.

Stories on to stages: adaptation and devising

If starting to devise without any text is too overwhelming to contemplate, you can always start to work with the words from a non-theatre text that you can adapt for performance. If your group has had little or no experience of creating their own texts, then finding a 'hook to hang things on', and working from a non-theatrical source is a good way to gain experience. Alternatively, a group of experienced, trained performers may also find the processes of devised adaptation offers them a new and stimulating way into making theatre (see Benmussa's comments on this point in Chapter 1, p. 11).

Of course, there are any number of writing sources you can adapt, but my detailed working example here is the adaptation of a short story. In any devising context, a frequently experienced difficulty is how to organise material; how to find a structure out of the many fragments of workshopped text. Adapting stories for the stage teaches us about techniques of shaping and communicating narratives, and helps us to acquire the confidence and skill to go on to create and to tell our own.

Adapting any short story requires finding a way of transposing the linguistic sign-system of the source text into the verbal and non-verbal communicating sign-systems of the theatre text. The processes of adaptation will require working from an understanding of what and how 'messages' are communicated in one, to examining the possibilities of what and how these are to be transposed and en-acted in the other. A key consideration in negotiating theatrical possibilities is the balance between the telling of the story and the way in which it is told. Finding a balance does not mean that there has to be an equal proportion of 'words' to 'images', but that there needs to be a working relation between the 'story' to be told and the means of telling. How a feminist register is to figure in the story and the telling is, of course, a fundamental theory–practice issue for us in this context.

Choosing a story to adapt

All members of your group should participate in choosing a story, rather than relying on one group member to find and to persuade the others of her choice. Although a time-consuming process, the group is likely to benefit in the long term as all members can feel they have taken part in a consultative process, and have shared in preliminary thoughts, aims and decision-making processes, and so on. In addition to library searches, your group might also try the 'elemental' object exercise (p. 147), which might help to recall important childhood stories. You may then wish to propose these for feminist revisioning, or, prompted by the past, you may then undertake further research to find feminist revisions of childhood tales (see the Resources section).

Each member of your group can be invited to circulate up to three choices of short story and to discuss their choices in the group giving an indication of their general appeal, and, more specifically, the feminist politics and pleasures that the stories afford, or, in the case of traditional tales, suggest they might be subjected to. Also include some beginning ideas about how you see the stories you have chosen being put into practice. Discussion about the theatrical shape a story might take in performance mode can be a lively and persuasive dynamic in early discussion stages: a visual sense of how a story might 'look' on stage helps generate energy, ideas and enthusiasm for potential projects. Table 1 in Chapter 7 (p. 126) can help with framing your thoughts about possible feminist aesthetics and performance registers.

Remember to ask your dramaturg to keep a record of your discussions. Notes from your preliminary discussion period will be useful to refer to (especially if ideas become blocked at any stage), even though original aims and decisions are highly likely to be modified as the work progresses.

Brainstorming: fairy tales and feminist tales

Once a group has decided on a story, it is useful to hold some brainstorming sessions aimed at sharing understandings of the story chosen for adaptation. One way of organising this is to set up three lines of enquiry. Looking at the short story use three separate sheets of paper to brainstorm:

1 narrative expectations and generic conventions of the short story;
2 feminist approaches in or to the story; and
3 implications of (1) and (2) for feminist performance.

Briefly, to expand on these three points:

1   entails asking questions of the text in order to develop a group awareness of its formal properties. Is the story a romance, a thriller, a fantasy? How do we know? What do we expect?

2   requires that the group focus on the feminist discourses of the story. Questions to be asked are what feminist positions are encoded in the text and how are they en-acted? If the text is not a feminist short story but is to be subjected to feminist enquiry, then what ideological concerns are the object of that enquiry?

3   Understandings derived from (1) and (2) will begin to shape initial ideas about form and ideology in relation to (3).

You will find it useful to build on your brainstorming with some practical work that continues to develop your awareness of the formal properties of the text in relation to the feminist project.

A simple, but highly effective exercise, is to workshop a traditional fairy story and its feminist counterpart. For example, Robson *et al.* suggest working as two groups to improvise a scene from a traditional tale and a scene from a feminist revisioning, and to counterpoint a 'soundtrack' (words and sounds) from one against the acting out of the other (Robson *et al.* 1990: 37). You could also try:

•   telling a traditional tale and inviting other women in your group to offer a different ending;
•   reading aloud a traditional tale and allowing your group to interrupt and to suggest a different action. You can try this verbally and physically;
•   acting out a traditional tale, but reversing gender roles;
•   story-boarding a conventional tale (e.g. in a freeze-framed sequence) and allowing characters to step out of the freeze-frame and say what they really think about themselves or about other characters in the frame.

What this kind of practical exploration will facilitate is critical thinking about agency and subject positioning. Bring this heightened awareness back to whatever story you are thinking of working on: are women the objects or subjects in the story? Are they empowered to 'act' or are actions done to them? What has to change if they are denied agency, and so on.

Story-lining, story-boarding

Trying to identify the key events, actions or moments that constitute the basic narrative of a story chosen for adaptation can help you to find a way of re-telling it in a theatrical context. The distinction between story and plot that the Russian formalists made is helpful to us here: the story is the basic narrative outline, which is shaped, re-told and re-ordered into the plot of a play, novel, short story, and so on. Try and identify a basic narrative chain of events and to story-board, on paper and in freeze-frames, the principal links in the chain. When you finally come to plot the links in your chain, these will probably appear in a very different order – but a simple story-line helps to show you what you have to work with.

Practical keys

When your group has a provisional narrative map and a sense of the feminist route on which (politically and aesthetically) it would like to travel, you can develop your work through the following kinds of body-writing proposals – always remembering to warm up voices and bodies before you begin on these project-related exercises.

Key lines of text

Each woman decides on a line that she feels is representative of a particular unit in the narrative chain. The line is explored vocally as a sequence of sounds, not words. Participants play with different sounds until satisfied with their sequence.

In a second stage women are invited to reduce the vocal sequence to just one sound that they feel is the key to the line. They should then focus on locating this sound in the body. Work on imaging the line of text can then begin by working out from the body-part focus discovered through vocal exploration. Having worked out a still, gestural image for the line, the sound can be put back in, and then the line itself.

Women should look for patterns of sounds and images within the group. If your group has a provisional narrative map of perhaps four or six links, work can proceed in this way for each link in order to develop a sound and image sequence for the narrative structure. This can be done both individually and collectively. You can play with these key lines in a number of physical and vocal ways: for example, orchestrating different sounds into collective image-making, or forming a chorus to one woman's sound–gesture–lines. As you experiment with these physical and vocal possibilities, also experiment with the sequencing of narrative links. What happens when the links appear in different orders?

Key images

Your group could work corporeally on imaging a particular link in the narrative chain. You might begin this by working individually, working in pairs and so on, until your whole group is working together. Look at points of similarity and contrast to see whether women have imaged a link quite differently, or have found gestures that seem to mirror or to echo each other. Take time to discuss what this tells you about your story, and so on. Try linear and simultaneous playing of the imaged links to heighten your awareness of their emotional highs and lows; their degrees of intensity or relief.

You can carry on with this work by looking at the visual possibilities of each link as each woman is invited to image her sequence of narrative links to change the focus, mood, emotion, intensity or shape of her image. The rest of the group can be her audience and can feed her suggestions: if a narrative link appears calm, what happens if she makes it look angry? As you alter the imaged links, you may see other stories emerging. Explore them and move out into other narrative chains.

Key objects

Each woman decides on an object that she sees as the key to a link in the narrative chain, and is given time to work individually with the object, exploring her emotional responses to it. As the work advances, key lines recorded from the first exercise can be fed into the explorations. The group can look at this individual work collectively, and feedback and discussion should be encouraged.

Create body sculptures around each object. The group could use the woman who has been working with a particular object to initiate the sculpture, and then other women could join in one by one. The first woman can then step out and physically mould the sculpture until she is satisfied with the image she has created. An object sculpture for each link can then be presented as a sequence. Simple linking movements could be choreographed to play through the sequence.

Body-writing into scripting

Beginning to body-write your short story along these lines (and see also the general suggestions in part one of this chapter), is one way of developing your own scripted performance. The key lines will help you to establish verbal motifs out of which to shape dialogue. It is often the case that devising workshops concentrate so overwhelmingly on image and body work that little attention is paid to developing the spoken text. Moreover, we should also note that writing dialogue is not necessarily a skill that we all have, and if we are devising collectively (as opposed to inviting a writer to adapt a text for us), then making use of lines taken directly from the text can be very helpful. Keeping records of key-line work-shopping will facilitate your more extensive adaptation of the text into the performance context.

At the same time, finding the words is also integral to finding the physical and aesthetic registers for the performer and the stage space. The image-based work helps the performer to find a means of story-telling through her body. Gestural rhythms can both inform the performance register and foreground or 'speak' key moments of action. With regard to the key objects, these may be used to orientate a spatial configuration of the playing space. Choreographing the links in the narrative chain can help to find positions for key objects. Additionally, other objects that participants might have noted as important to a link, but were not selected as their key object, can also be added into the space in a way which begins to shape and to define a playing space.

Case study: *The Bloody Chamber*

I wish to conclude with a brief case study of a student adaptation of Angela Carter's *The Bloody Chamber* as a way of illustrating and consolidating the working methods outlined in this chapter.

Briefly, for the reader who is not familiar with this short story, the tale is as follows. A mother and her daughter are parted by the daughter's marriage to an elderly widower – a patriarchal figure who reminds the daughter of her own dead father. In the voyeuristic gaze of the husband, represented as sadist and pornographer, the heroine is put to the test. The (father) husband commands that she resist the temptation of unlocking the bloody chamber, which contains the bodies of his previous three wives, all killed by his own hand. When she fails to resist this temptation, he proposes to kill her, too. The sadistic pleasure of her death is, however, thwarted by the intervention of the mother. Although it is the mother who gives away her daughter in marriage, it is also the mother who rescues and reclaims her daughter from (marriage) death by killing the patriarch. The closure of the tale reverses the traditional rags to riches narrative, and Carter's heroine marries a blind piano-tuner who helped in her rescue – a man who without sight does not have the power to 'gaze'.

A devising group of three women students workshopped a short (15-minute) adaptation of *The Bloody Chamber*, developing their narrative line through the kinds of physical imaging, key lines and object play described in this chapter.[2] The group elected to involve two women in the performance and to appoint one woman as director and dramaturg. (Remember: how your group works will of course be determined by group size and gender. A mixed group might wish to introduce patriarchal figure/s, etc., or a larger group of women might choose to work collectively on the different roles – see *Portraits of Rossetti*, Chapter 9, p. 167).

The women elected to script the performance as a two-hander shared between mother and daughter. The story-line was shaped, plotted through the bodies of the two women performers. Both women had to play out the oppressive realm of the father performed on and through the body, but the continued absent/present body of the maternal functioned as a subversive presence threatening to break through, pressing on the symbolic realm of the father/husband.

The director helped the performers to find a physical style of playing by extensive workshopping of paired image work. In the first narrative link, for instance, the bodies were mapped together; were as one, in continuous, contiguous gestural patterns. Entry into the patriarchal/symbolic (link two), however, marked a change in paired movement as the daughter was forced to survey the boundary of her own body, 'a-part' from her mother. As the action developed and the narrative of masculinist desire was played out and through the female body, the opposition between the symbolic and the semiotic registered in tensions between different body parts. For example, pain (symbolic) was taken in through the pelvis to the stomach and womb, whilst pleasure (semiotic) was encoded in an opposite movement in which hands and fingertips stretched out.

The verbal text was woven into the physical text and was largely worked out by marking up key lines in a copy of the short story, which were then activated through body-writing. Two main functions of the words were: (1) the telling of the narrative chain of events to progress the action; and (2) the 'captioning' or underscoring of visual moments. For example, rape imagery was set against the key line 'a dozen husbands impaled a dozen brides'. Workshopping also made use of words to alienate the visual. The story tells, for instance, of how the heroine is left a number of keys in her care. The linguistic reference to a number of keys was counterpointed with the imaging of just one key: the key to the bloody chamber. Or, the description of the undressing of the bride in the gaze of the husband, was spoken against the putting on, rather than the taking off, of the costume or masquerade of 'femininity'. These workshopped ideas encouraged a 'not…but' style of playing, which resisted the objectified si(gh)ting of the body-feminine.

The daughter's entry into the symbolic was marked by her climbing into the wedding dress and by her confrontation of three other dresses, each representing one of the three dead wives. This metonymic substitution critiqued the systems of representation that position women as objects to be looked at and encoded the gaze of the sadist/pornographer. Improvisational play with the dresses – responding to texture, colour, style, etc. (see 'fabricating words' exercise, p. 146) – was the base on which these sequences were built. As the workshopping developed, the director and performers found positions for each of the dresses, which they returned to in order to choreograph movement. These were eventually used to define the playing space. Other key object-play centred on a red choker ('splits' mind from body and prefigures the destiny of the heroine), and a metronome, which substituted for the daughter's piano playing, and marked the linear time of the symbolic before the daughter is released into the rescuing, monumental time of the maternal. As a short, workshopped presentation, the aim was not to encourage the use of lavish technical resources. Hence, in addition to the few key objects, the setting was created by making use of what was already available in the playing space: black drapes re-hung to enclose the audience into the space/'chamber', rostra for playing levels, and colour projections on to the cyclorama (red for the chamber; blue for the sea (mer) or mother (mère)).

In short, what was realised through this devised feminist adaptation was a lucid narrative line carried through an aesthetic register appropriate to Carter's central A-effect: the alienation of the sadistic narrative of masculinist desire.

RESOURCES

Angela Carter's *The Bloody Chamber* (Harmondsworth: Penguin, 1979) is the title story of a revisionist collection that includes versions of *Red Riding Hood*, *Sleeping Beauty*, and *Beauty and the Beast*. (The *Red Riding Hood* revision, *The Company of Wolves*, was made into a film (1984), which might also be helpful for thinking about feminist adaptations, albeit in a different medium.) I recommend Carter's writing for adaptation because you will find that her style of magic realism, using the fantastic to defamiliarise our expectations of the realistic, lends itself to the medium of theatre, which trades in the illusion of the real and the real as illusion, and to a feminist theatre practice, creatively and politically committed to the alienation of the 'real'.

Additionally Carter has also edited two volumes of fairy tales for Virago Press, *The Virago Book of Fairy Tales* (London:Virago, 1990) and *The Second Virago Book of Fairy Tales* (London: Virago, 1992), which may be useful sources for workshopping. You might also like to try Suniti Namjoshi's *Feminist Fables* (London: Sheba, 1981).

A number of mainstream and women's publishing houses issue short story collections that focus on women writers. *Women Writers of the Fin-de-Siècle* edited by Elaine Showalter (London: Virago, 1993), or *Infinite Riches: Modern Classics – Short Stories* edited by Lynn Knight (London:Virago, 1993) might be good places to start looking.

Chapter 9

Re-figuring lives

In this, and the following chapter, I wish to focus on women's lives as a subject for devising. My concluding chapter looks specifically at working with our selves as the subject/s of the feminist devising process, while here I am principally concerned with the lives of other women: working with the possibilities of feminist biography, rather than autobiography. At the outset of this study we noted Alison Oddey's observation, 'devised theatre can start from anything' (Oddey 1994: 1), and this being the case I found it difficult to decide which devising projects to share in this part of the volume. However my attention to women's lives in this and the final chapter arises from the ways in which they touch centrally on the principal concerns of many woman-centred projects: representation of the self/selves, the (de-)construction of social and cultural identities, and the question of 'truth'. My proposals in this chapter are illustrated by a brief case study of a devised performance based on the life and writings of the poet Christina Rossetti.

Feminist biography: theory and practice

It may be helpful for you as women theatre-makers to begin by thinking about biographies you have read and enjoyed, to make a note (perhaps in a brainstorming session) of what these are and what the biographical pleasures were. For example, were you fascinated by the subject? Is this someone who is important to your own life, or someone you admire, or would like to be like? Did you get to the bottom of a biographical 'truth'. Did you find a new bit of a biographical jigsaw puzzle? Did it tell a good story?

When looking for biographical subjects to work on, remember that possible women subjects are not necessarily in 'view'. From the outset of this study we have commented on the obscuration of women's social, creative and theatrical histories, so finding a subject may be linked to the project of making the 'invisible' visible. This may, for example, mean moving away from published sources and discovering 'subjects' through letters, diaries, oral histories or parish records.

Agreeing on a biographical subject to work on may be a difficult task if the group puts forward a wide range of suggestions, so a few brainstorming sessions may be needed to arrive at a decision. As in the short story example in the last chapter, your group should be aware of why you have chosen your figure (subject), what feminist possibilities you feel she offers, and how you see your selected figure in practical terms. Also, the entire group should be involved in taking a look at feminist approaches to biography. Your dramaturg could be invited to research relevant publications and bring these to the attention of your group for shared study.

You may find it helpful to explore possible criteria for a feminist biographical practice, or, indeed, to ask yourselves whether such a practice exists. Finding examples of biographical writing that you think is feminist in approach is one way of tackling this. As you share biographical examples that you wish to argue are feminist, think specifically about *how* a biographical practice works; what makes it feminist in your view? Look across a range of examples in your group and see if you can begin to find any patterns, and to consider these in conjunction with any feminist theory sources provided by your dramaturg.

One feminist study of biography which may be useful to you for devising is Liz Stanley's *The Auto/biographical I*. Commenting on the relative conservatism of biography, compared to autobiography, Stanley writes:

> reconstructing feminism from them [feminist biographies], a reader would conclude that apart from the interest in female and/or feminist subjects, feminist biography is in many respects conventional and indistinguishable from the best products of the mainstream, following the conventions of genre rather than challenging them.
>
> (Stanley 1992: 248)

That said, Stanley proceeds with four proposals for a biography which might 'challenge' the 'conventional'; for making a biography feminist:

- anti-spotlight;
- contingent;
- anti-realist; and
- foregrounding textually-located ideological practices.

(Stanley 1992: 253)

According to Stanley, these four elements offer a 'method' and a 'form' for producing feminist 'auto/biography'. (Stanley's proposals are discussed in relation to both biography and autobiography, so this commentary might be useful for framing ideas in Chapter 10.) Let us look at how these four elements might offer us a means of creating a feminist biography through theatrical practice.

Anti-spotlight

Working away from or de-centring the individual as the subject of biography, may seem at odds with biographical writing that tradition-ally spotlights the 'great' or exceptional single figure (Stanley 1992: 253). On the other hand, an anti-spotlight ethos is common to femi-nist thinking, organisation and creativity. If you accept the anti-spotlight as a feminist proposal, there are two key ways in which you might begin to respond:

- By presenting a group or a community of women as the biographical subject.
- By subjecting the individual in the spotlight to deconstructive feminist play.

Your dramaturg could be invited to bring plays to the group that show you examples of both of these in a dramatic context. For instance, you might look at Sarah Daniels's *The Gut Girls*, which stages a working-class community of women working in meat sheds in Deptford at the turn of the century (Daniels: 1994), or biograph-ical single-figure plays by Pam Gems. Gems works on 'great' figures such as Edith Piaf or Queen Christina, but with a view to re-figuring or demythologising these famous women (see the Resources section for further suggestions).

The following sections indicate practical ways in which you can being to explore anti-spotlight strategies.

Spotlight on the 'ordinary'

Place an ordinary woman in the spotlight, so that the 'ordinary' critiques the convention of the 'extraordinary'. Daniels, for example, creates monologues for disempowered women in her plays, which are used to cut across other narratives (see p. 109). Find out what happens if you put an 'ordinary' woman in the spotlight to tell her story? What does she want to say? What are her stories?

Cross-class contests

If you have a 'great' ('high-status') figure to work on, create an ordinary ('low-status') figure to play opposite her. For example, take an episode from your subject's life, have her speak about it and use your invented character to interrupt, challenge or quiz her. Improvise the dialogue and keep a record. You might also try finding oppositional movements for the two figures (subjects) through paired physical play, which is also useful for intrafeminine explorations of class- and gender-related conflict.

Missing subjects

Try improvising a biographical scene from your subject's life, and then replay the scene without her present. Your group could be invited to re-play the scene in reporting mode, talking about what 'they' said and what 'she' said. See how the words of your missing subject are reported; how her 'story' is retold by others in her absence. Remember, biographies are always someone else's 'stories' about other people's lives.

Unpicking the moment

Try improvising a 'famous' scene in the life of your subject, and freezing the action at a critical moment for your subject to thought-track her feelings, views, reactions, across the scene. For example, a number of biographical 'greats' die in mysterious circumstances (Marilyn Monroe, or, more recently, Princess Diana). The public are offered a representation of that moment – through biographies, the media, etc. – but find out what your subject might like to say in her 'own' words.

Collective subject

If you are working on a single figure try using a number of performers to 'be' your figure: she is played by your group, not just by one woman. Resistance to performer–subject identification is a way of de-centring the notion of 'great' subject (see the Rossetti case study, p. 167).

Contingent

It may be helpful to expand on this second element of feminist biography. Stanley writes:

> The content of what counts as 'knowledge' in feminist and cultural political terms needs to be shifted; the act of socialising biography de-centres the subject....Founded upon this social rather than individualist approach, a distinct feminist biography textually recognises that its facts and arguments are contingent. That is, it recognises that biographical as any other writing is produced from a particular view point, that of the busily inscribing author.
>
> (Stanley 1992: 250)

In our theatre practice we can use a 'social rather than an individualist' approach to re-present a biographical subject from a particular materialist viewpoint. In such a practice our focus is not the telling of an individual woman's story but the social, material production of that individual, or community of individuals.

To work with a social rather than an individualist approach, you will need to include research into the material conditions of the life or lives of the woman/women you are presenting and to activate this research through materialist–feminist techniques (see Chapter 7, Table 1, p. 126 for a quick reminder). The following sections contain some practical suggestions for how you might go about this.

A room of one's own

Research the spaces in which your biographical subject lived. You might consider photographs of places, houses or rooms and begin to understand the social 'text' of those locations. Did your subject have, as Virginia Woolf describes it, a room of her own for writing, creating, living? Or did she share with children, sisters, a mother, women servants? Is she socially empowered or disempowered in a particular location? Improvise your subject's space. Find out whether this is her space. Who has access to it? Can she lock the door? How does she feel in it, or how would she like to feel in it.

Daily rituals

Use your social research to find out what the daily domestic rituals might have been for your subject. Play these out in a choreographed, physical sequence, constantly repeating actions to develop a feeling for whatever the domestic ritual might be. This kind of work can form a useful base for developing a 'chorus' of movement in scenes – as a backdrop to a special biographical moment in an otherwise dull, daily routine, perhaps. You can also incorporate sounds and key words into your movement patterns.

Family portraits

Find photographs of your subject's family and friends. Stage the photographs yourselves and look at the social grouping for status, relationships, etc. Try moving your subject around the photograph you have set up. Find out how this affects her 'image'. Are there people she can stand next to, be close to, or has to back away from because she cannot bear to be near them? In your explorations, try to think further about these portraits in the wider social context to which they belong, and the implications of status and relations when you take account of this.

Parallel texts, parallel lives

In researching material about the social conditions affecting women during the lifetime of your subject, look out for (or ask your dramaturg to look out for) accounts that you can work from to create a parallel text in a devised biographical scene. You may be improvising a biographical moment that is individualist in approach, but may be creatively counterpointed with a social commentary. For example: imagine you are working on a subject living in a time when childbirth is dangerous for women. Perhaps your subject gives an account of a painful, but successful delivery that you interrupt, juxtapose or play against a different social narration detailing the conditions of childbirth for women at the time.

Anti-realist

> Anti-realism   disrupts   chronology   and   periodisation.…Anti-realism…confounds the certainties of the reader, pulls away all that can be pulled from under our collective readerly feet. We end with one certainty: that lives are not simple.
>
> (Stanley 1992: 252–3)

I shall not go over the anti-realist impulse of our modern feminist theatre practice, which, by now, needs very little introduction as the arguments have been well-rehearsed throughout this volume. I need no persuading of this third element for staging a feminist biography (although this may be a point of discussion in your groups). If you are engaging in a materialist practice – possibly, for example, using some of the techniques described under 'contingent' – then your style of working is likely to take you away from a linear, chronological realistic approach. I would like to extend this by sharing possibilities of 'anti-realist' ways of creating a biographical structure, or rather 'anti-structure'.

Quilting

Instead of thinking about a biographical chronology, think about the life of your subject as a patchwork quilt: recycled bits of material that you can put together in changing patterns of colour and texture. We found this a particularly useful image for thinking about structure when working on a devised presentation on the life and writings of Susan Glaspell.[1] Not until we were close to the moment of showing the work were we clear about how the 'patches' we had made might 'fit' together in performance. Nor, in our anti-realist mode, were we trying to hide the 'seams'.

If you are working in a collective devising mode (as we were in the Glaspell Project) you can share the responsibility for creating individual 'patches' out of particular biographical episodes, and then playing with possibilities of how these might fit together much later. If you are showing work, then at a later stage it might be useful for your group to appoint a woman to direct/'sew' the 'quilt' into some sort of 'final' shape for showing.

Whose memory?

There is little we can be certain of in biographical 'truth' other than the complexity of a life. You may find it productive to spend some time looking at different accounts of your biographical subject and her very different representations. Try taking different accounts of a key episode and staging and re-staging a scene which dramatises this episode according to the different accounts you have found (you may even like to layer in your own imagined accounts of the episode). In your playing, treat all of the accounts even-handedly; try not to make one seem more credible or 'truthful' than another. Use these as a kind of chorus or motif that is repeated or patterned through other scenes; as a means of refusing linear playing or 'fixing' your subject.

Textually located ideological practices

Working physically with 'textually located' words offers the possibility of foregrounding ways in which biographical texts might be used to 'fix' a particular subject. 'Unfixing' a subject through the kinds of theory–practice suggestions presented here, means that we can resist, refuse or reinvent the way our subject has been presented through a particular biographical 'script', and can draw our attention to the formal and ideological properties of different kinds of scripting, through our feminist biographical theatre practice.

'Transtextual' practice

In performance we are free to play across a range of texts, resourced from biographical materials and from our imaginations, and offer these back to our spectators. As we juxtapose one kind of 'text' with another, we create the possibility of 'seeing' or exposing the ideological practices at work in each text. For example, in the case of biographical subjects who are writers, an effective transtextual practice is to blend together works of fiction with the 'fictions' of the writer's life.

The feminist critic

Inventing a figure to play the role of a feminist critic 'walking' through all the biographical material and trying to find her 'subject' can be a playful workshopping device (and a possibility for building into a devised performance). A figure identified as a feminist critic offers a clear, contingent viewpoint, and is well placed to challenge and to unpick the representations of her subject in textual sources.

Portraits of Rossetti

To help make further sense of the theory–practice suggestions I have outlined in this chapter, I propose to re-visit Stanley's four elements through a case study example of a devised project based on the writing and life of the poet Christina Rossetti.[2] For this project we worked across a range of textual and visual sources, which included Rossetti's own writings, biographical accounts of her life and Pre-Raphaelite art. The six women taking part worked as devising-performers, using their skills in body-writing, while the task of finding textual sources and starting to re-shape or to script these for performance fell to myself as principal dramaturg. I would suggest that if you do work in a similar way on this kind of feminist biographical theatre project, that you do appoint at least one, if not two, women to the role of dramaturg, in order for your group to stay on top of the source materials.

Our key aim on the Rossetti project was the re-presentation of the figure of Christina Rossetti; a re-presentation that would enable her to take up a subject position in her own narrative. This would involve de-stablising the identity or representation of the woman poet as 'fixed' in the (fictional) narratives of family, friends and critical voices, both contemporary and modern. We agreed to explore a feminist–materialist practice that would steer us away from the risk of sentimentalising the 'great' poet, and which would enable us to examine the social and cultural conditions for a woman writing in the nineteenth century.

We decided on the representation of Rossetti as a collective subject: all six women working on the project would be part of the Rossetti figure. In dramatic terms, we agreed that this meant disrupting any tendency to work in a linear narrative structure: to resist telling a biographical story from birth to death. Rather than work towards a linear, causally related sequence of scenes, we proposed to shape material into an episodic montage of portraits. This gave us the title *Portraits of Rossetti*, which we hoped might index the ambiguity of authorship: whose portraits are these? Christina as presented and imaged by whom, for whom? The concept of the portrait came from looking at the Pre-Raphaelite paintings, especially those of Christina's brother,

Dante Gabriel Rossetti, and the Pre-Raphaelite imaging of women. As art historian Jan Marsh states, 'if there is one image that conveys the idea of Pre-Raphaelite art it is that of a woman's face, set with large, lustrous eyes and surrounded by a mass of loose hair, looking soulfully out of the canvas' (Marsh 1985: 1).

There were two workshopping techniques that helped us to work on the social and cultural oppression of Rossetti: the use of games and playing with opposites. At first, using games seemed to be just an extension of warm-up and concentration exercises. Gradually, however, they were used more extensively as a means of exploring the competitive side to Rossetti, which, allegedly, she spent her life seeking to repress and control. By using different games in which the group conspires to prevent a particular individual from winning, we were able to work on emotions of frustration and anger. Out of this kind of exploration we were eventually able to devise pieces that examined gender-based frustrations of repressive social conditioning. Some of the game-playing was carried through from the workshopping into the devised presentation. For example, an aggressive game of musical chairs formed the basis for an image which demonstrated how Christina, although desiring to reach a 'chair' first, could never win against her brother Dante Gabriel.

The need to repress passionate or uncontrollable emotions that did not sit happily with the image of the 'proper' Victorian 'lady' also provided the impetus for working with opposites, and was a further means of exploring the 'fixing' and 'unfixing' of subjectivity and representation. The contradictions between the desire to create, to write and en-gendered social conditioning were workshopped physically through explorations of gestural opposites. For example, paired work explored the controlled versus the passionate body, and the opposing gestural patterns that created a site of conflict. In the performance, for example, this work was used to create a self-wounding image in which Rossetti 'cut' her arms with a pair of scissors (a motif based on an incident in Rossetti's adolescent life).

We turned Rossetti herself into a kind of modern-day feminist critic: bringing her back to 'life' so that she could look at and interrogate her textual (mis)-representations. An increasingly disgruntled Rossetti flicked through anthologies of poetry to find out how many entries she had, or grew increasingly outraged by the various 'epitaphs' heaped on her after her death. All of the portraits interrogated biographical 'truths', contextualised by social realities, without ever arriving at a single 'truth'.

Portrait Five, entitled 'Sisterhood', staged a meeting between Christina Rossetti and the painter Elizabeth Siddal, who eventually married Dante Gabriel Rossetti. Whereas biographies give accounts of hostilities between these two women, who apparently rarely met, our portrait staged an imagined, interrogative scene in which 'distance' between the two women was gradually overcome. The vehicle for exploring this was Rossetti's probing of the mythologisation of the artist's model, which is how Lizzie Siddal is most commonly remembered, rather than as an artist in her own right. In this way, both women became the subjects of this portrait; both were drawn into the biographical sketch of two women striving for creative lives, while living through an historical moment of social and cultural oppression. The play between 'image' and 'reality' was enacted through the counterpointing of linguistic and visual registers. For example, the opening to the portrait was played against a slide of Millais's painting *Ophelia*, undercut by the dialogue, which 'painted' a different picture:

Christina: You had your painting.
Lizzie: My painting! Who remembers my painting! I'm Ophelia in the bathtub who almost died of pneumonia.
Christina: Was it dreadfully chilly?
Lizzie: It was when the oil lamps went out and that bastard Millais never noticed until I was half dead with cold.

The portrait went on to suggest points of contact between the two women: their struggles to lead creative lives; the ways in which illness was used as an argument against their creativity; the domineering and threatening (male) presence of Dante Gabriel.

Stanley concludes that working with the four elements she proposes will 'encourage active reading' (Stanley 1992: 255). Similarly, I would conclude that working on the Rossetti project, in a de-centred, transtextual 'quilting' or patching together of portraits encouraged spectators to engage in a feminist re-figuring of Rossetti. The invitation to the spectator was not to look, but to look again.

RESOURCES

Playwright Pam Gems has written a number of biographical plays with subjects as wide-ranging as Marlene Dietrich and Stanley

Spencer. For the de-mythologising of 'great' figures try Pam Gems's *Piaf* in *Three Plays* (Harmondsworth: Penguin, 1985), or *Queen Christina*, in M. Remnant, *Plays By Women: Five* (London: Methuen, 1986).

Other dramatisations of biographical figures by contemporary women playwrights that you may find useful to consult include: Edna O'Brien's biographical dramatisation of Virginia Wolf, *Virginia* (London: Hogarth, 1981); Anna Furse's re-presentation of Charcot's patient, Augustine (see p. 70), *Augustine* (Amsterdam: Harwood, 1997), and Liz Lochhead's treatment of Mary Shelley in *Blood and Ice*, in M. Wandor (ed.) *Plays by Women: Four* (London: Methuen, 1985), and her re-presentation of Mary Queen of Scots and Elizabeth 1 in *Mary Queen of Scots Got Her Head Chopped Off* (Harmondsworth: Penguin, 1987).

Also of interest is Rose Leiman Goldemberg's *Letters Home* in M. Wandor (ed.) *Plays by Women: Two* (London: Methuen, 1983), which stages a biographical duet between Sylvia Plath and her mother, Aurelia, working from Sylvia's letters as a source. *Dear Girl*, by Tierl Thompson and Libby Mason, in E. Aston and G. Griffin (eds) *Herstory: Two* (Sheffield: Sheffield Academic Press, 1991), is an example of a woman-centred play working from a diary source to present a community of four 'ordinary' women – Ruth Slate, Eva Slawson, Minna Simmons and Françoise Lafitte – who lived in the early part of this century.

Julie Wilkinson's two-hander, *Mrs. Beeton's History of the World*, in *Contemporary Theatre Review*, 1997, vol. 6, no. 3, uses the imaginary figure of Caroline, Isabella Beeton's maid-of-all work, to probe her mistress's account of biographical events. The same volume also contains Foursight Theatre's collectively devised *Bloody Mary and the Virgin Queen*, which comically re-presents the lives of Elizabeth I and her sister Mary Tudor. Foursight have specialised in devising and commissioning new work on female biographical subjects.

An insightful essay on dramatisations of women writers is Anita Plath Helle's 'Re-presenting women writers on stage: a retrospective to the present' in L. Hart (ed.) *Making a Spectacle* (Ann Arbor: University of Michigan Press, 1989), pp. 195–208.

Stanley (1992) has an extensive bibliography on feminist auto/biography that you will find useful for further research sources. See also the Resources section accompanying Chapter 10.

Chapter 10

Performing your selves

Using yourselves as creative agents in the making of feminist performance has been the principal focus of this study. In this final chapter, I should like to offer some suggestions for a feminist theatre practice in which you make use of your 'selves' not only as the agents but as the subjects of performance. Moreover, I should like to conclude by showing how a mode of autobiographical devising may also serve as a way of discovering and defining feminism. Practical proposals in this chapter are illustrated with reference to two devised projects: (1) on the theme of mothers by daughters and (2) on the subject of growing up in the Thatcher years.

'The personal is political'

Academic study tends to drive us away from ourselves: 'far from encouraging our ability to think creatively about discovering the truths in personal narratives, our academic disciplines have more often discouraged us from taking people's life stories seriously' (Personal Narratives Group, 1989: 262). To think of ourselves as a (feminist) subject for theatre studies alongside Shakespeare, Miller or Brecht seems incongruous. We need to find ways of 'taking people's life stories seriously', or rather 'women's life stories seriously', as a subject for theatre-making and academic study.

One way of beginning to re-think this, is to re-state and re-work the belief, shared by women in the 1970s Women's Liberation Movement (WLM), that 'the personal is political'. In the 1970s the WLM created a context for (mainly middle-class) women to look at their lives; to see that 'the personal is political' as a way of raising political consciousness and changing lives. In the 1990s there is no comparable feminist movement, but this allows you the possibility of self-defining feminism through an exploration of what is individually and collectively oppressive to you as young women.

In her discussion of feminism and 'the project of using autobiography politically' (which you might think of as an umbrella title for the kinds of ideas and projects put forward in this chapter), Julia Swindells states two basic premises that are useful to keep as points of reference to come back to:

1   'to articulate the experience of oppression first-hand is a precondition for social and political change'; and
2   'collective testimony is one of the best means of achieving this, so that neither author nor reader [spectator] sees the autobiographical project as a matter of individualism'.

(Swindells 1995: 213)

Autobiography, feminism and theatre

Before embarking on your own devising, one of the research tasks your group might undertake is a shared search for examples of the autobiographical used in contemporary women's performance.

Autobiographical discourse is most clearly marked in work by women performance artists that combines a first–person narrative with the real life presence of the performing 'self'. As Claire MacDonald describes:

> when a performance artist stands up in front of an audience she is assumed to be performing as herself. By putting her own body and her own experience forward within a live space the artist becomes both object and subject within the work.

(MacDonald 1995: 189)

Try making your own study of how such an artist performs 'as herself'. A good example to take is Bobby Baker (see the Resources section). In performances such as *Kitchen Show* or *Drawing on A Mother's Experience*, Baker explores 'the personal is the political' by performing details of her life as an ordinary housewife and a mother. This personal detail is politicised in her work as the representation of professional and private 'selves', the artist and housewife–mother, and makes visible the divisions women experience in their lives between work and family. In the Mothers by Daughters Project I describe later, a group viewing of *Drawing on a Mother's Experience* generated a spontaneous discussion about mothers. In particular, Baker's device of 'drawing' with food triggered a number of images and stories women had around mothers and food in their families. The group made a note of these, and was subsequently able to workshop ideas from this initial discussion (see later).

One further example of a solo performer whom you may find useful to study, because of her focus on gender politics, is Claire Dowie (see Resources section). Dowie's use of first-person narratives in her self-styled 'stand-up theatre plays' invites audiences into auto-biographical 'readings' or 'spectatings': 'when Dowie plays the part her cropped hair, slight figure, and rather tomboyish appearance suggest that the story she is telling is an autobiographical one' (Rose 1995: 32–3). (The autobiographical assumption may be false, as, for example, in Dowie's stand-up monologue, *Adult Child/Dead Child*, which she vehemently declares is not based on herself, but the invitation to associate between material and performer comes from the first-person narrative and style of delivery.) Working through a style of anarchic comedy, Dowie uses her different selves to 'trouble' gender. In *Why is John Lennon Wearing a Skirt?*, for example, she uses the central *Gestus* of the skirt in her first-person narrative of a young girl, often mistaken for a boy, whose hero is John Lennon of the 'Fab Four', to foreground women's oppression (Dowie 1996).

Of particular interest to you are the ways in which gender confusion is encoded in Dowie's playwriting: a clash of registers between stand-up comedy and 'theatre plays', which mirrors the 'misfit' impulse of her first-person narratives of gender displacement and identity confusion. Using examples of Dowie's work as your point of reference, the women in your group could think about their own teenage narratives and 'misfit' experiences.

The 'uses of autobiography' in group performances may be less immediately obvious, but if you target your research at companies who make use of devising in some way and invite performers to make an active contribution to the writing processes, you are likely to come across further examples of the autobiographical that may be helpful to bring to your group. For example, in the making of Caryl Churchill's *Cloud Nine* (see Chapter 2, p. 29), the Joint Stock company who originally worked on the play in the late 1970s were invited to use themselves and their sexual politics as part of the workshopping processes. (You can find some examples of their work-shopping techniques in Ritchie 1987.)

Companies with a commitment to sexual politics such as Gay

Sweatshop, Split Britches (see Case 1996) or DV8 are likely to be useful to you. When you bring in examples, try and think about how the autobiographical is marked in a performance What interests you about this? What should your group take note of, think about and work with? For example, DV8 may refer to each other in performances by their own names. What are the effects of self-naming? How might you see your group using this technique? What ideological work would you want it to do?

Proposal for a structure

Thinking through the 'uses of autobiography' available to you as examples in solo and group performances, and noting in particular the focus on gender, will help with framing a devising model which combines aspects of both of these: one in which first-person narratives specific to individual women may be woven into a collective autobiographical narrative.

In print culture, an equivalent model for this might be the generational collection of autobiographical stories. Virago, for example, has published several of these, which you could look at (see the Resources section). Where written examples of this kind of model require sequential organisation – stories are set out one after the other – performance creates the possibility of simultaneous narrative play. Think about your structure as the collective weaving together of the individual stories of a generation of young women who grew up in the Thatcher years. As the authoring of your autobiographical text is plural not singular, your impulse will be towards multiplicity, discontinuity, rupture, fragmentation and away from the singular, the continuous, the linear and the whole. As a group working on 'the personal is political', think about bringing both performers and audiences to a political awareness of the social text in which your stories are personally, culturally and materially located as part of your aims.

Also, think about this collective structuring of the autobiographical as a structure for working. In order to make this piece about all of, or out of all of, the women in your group, think about sharing the responsibility of developing material. One way to divide this up is for each woman to take responsibility for a segment of work that means the most to her. Allowing women the space to work on and to take the lead in strands of performance that they feel most strongly about, or attached to, can often prove the most productive way to generate performance material.

Autobiography in the workshop

While researching and thinking about a structure to work in, you can begin to include some basic workshopping on the theme of autobiography. Here are some general, practical suggestions for getting started.

In beginning autobiographical work, all group members need to feel that they can trust the group with their stories; it is important the everyone understands that all stories have equal importance and validity. You can make introductions general, or you can give them a specific focus, depending upon the autobiographical project you have in mind. However, it is useful to think about using introductions as a way of finding out the kind of detail that a group needs to be aware of for participants to feel comfortable: if you are going to be working on mothers and daughters, then does every woman in your group have a mother who is still living, for example?

Introducing yourselves

Women being presented with the idea that they are going to produce autobiographical monologues would make for an intimidating beginning, whereas confidence can be generated in your group through monologue-making warm-ups, which require minimal spotlighting of individuals.

- As a very simple way of beginning, your group could work in pairs. A tells her story to B, who tells it back to A, and *vice versa*. This story-telling reversal could be repeated, but with the whole group sitting in a circle to listen.
- Again with the group sitting in a circle, each woman takes it in turn to introduce herself. After the initial round of introductions is complete the introductions are repeated but using sounds rather than words, and playing with (1) exaggerated, (2) minimal and (3) frozen gestures while vocalising. This can be a fun way of raising an awareness of how we use our bodies when talking: are you someone who has to use their hands, who moves their head a lot and so on?
- 'How to be a woman': features in women's magazines that advise on how to be the best girl, housewife, mother, bride and so on, can be useful both as icebreakers and for generating material. To give an example: find a list of 'true' advice for women readers.

One that offered advice from mums on boyfriends, for instance, listed comments such as 'He's not right for you', 'You'll get over him' or 'He'll never leave her'. Your group can quickly move on by coming up with examples of their own: advice that their own mothers or primary carers have given them. Participants can then be invited to give a response to the advice – often what they would like to say but dare not say. They can then be invited to respond to advice other than their own, building advice and response patterns so that whoever responds to a piece of advice then has to keep the momentum going by offering some advice of their own, thereby generating a quick exchange. While this kind of task helps to put women at their ease, your group can at this stage also begin to develop narrative lines by inviting each woman to share, briefly, in the autobiographical story that occasioned the advice. Use this kind of play to look at ideologies of femininity. Question, for example, the (frequently) presumed heterosexuality. Examine your own lives in relation to feminine fictions, and so on.

•   Think about Claire Dowie's skirt as an example of 'how to be', or similar items of clothing from your past that trigger associations of gender behaviour and restrictions. See what you can find in your own wardrobes. Bring an item of clothing in to the group, and discuss how you felt about wearing it, what it represented, and how you felt 'inside' it. If your group is working well together, is supportive and confident, you may feel able to offer spontaneous improvisations using the clothing.

Photographs

Photographs are an invaluable source for generating personal narratives. Each snapshot has a story, or rather several stories to tell. Photographs are personal and often highly emotionally charged, so you will need to think carefully about making a selection to work with.

A supportive atmosphere is essential for women to make public private representations of themselves, their family, their friends and so on. Make sure that everyone agrees and is comfortable about bringing in photographs. You can do this by having a group discussion about how you feel about being photographed, by each woman describing the worst photograph of themselves, the occasion when it was taken, and so on. Here are some examples.

- School photographs. Share the memories these invite and try writing captions or even brief monologues to accompany them.
- Special occasion photographs (for example, of a birthday, Christmas, and so on). Talk about how you felt, what the photograph does not image (on special occasions we collude in representing ourselves in a particular way — how is a your photograph posed? Did the camera 'lie'?).
- Family albums. These might be your own, or they might belong to another member of your family. What stories do they tell. If the album is put together by another member of your family, does it tell a different story to your own? Are there narratives you like, or dislike? Is there a favourite page of images?

Photo-histories, diaries and stories: Jo Spence

Photographer Jo Spence (see Chapter 5) wrote some excellent essays on the kind of work you can do with photography and family albums. In particular, Spence offers practical advice for work you can begin on your own in private: creating your own 'self-histories' out of different periods of your life, or keeping 'photo-diaries' of your current lives (Spence 1995: 192 5). You could undertake this work individually and privately, as Spence suggests, and, subsequently, select from this work whatever you feel confident about and able to share with your group.

Spence also offers the idea of working on photo-stories for girls. She suggests making your own that subvert dominant ideologies of teenage femininity — another 'how to be/not to be' exercise (Spence 1995: 68). To do this, try the following kinds of activity.

- Find a photo-story in a girl's magazine and act it out reversing gender roles, or changing the ending.
- Try creating your own freeze-frames of the stills. Look at them and see what you want to change.
- Or, simulate the freeze-frames and make your own cartoon bubbles on large sheets of paper, but write captions for them that dislocate the images, and so on.

Personal objects — Cristina Castrillo

Set aside some time to improvise regularly with an object to which you have a strong emotional attachment. This kind of exercise is included in the actor-training programme of Cristina Castrillo, which aims to develop the control (physical memory) of the performer with the personal (emotional memory). Working privately on objects in your group (each woman finds her own space to work in, concentrating solely on her own object, her own improvisational play), is a way of encouraging the emotional memory to surface. Working on this repeatedly helps you to develop the skill to, eventually, show this within the group, and maybe even to include it in performance.

Case study 1: *Imaging the Link*: mothers by daughters

The practical suggestions, observations and advice that follow in this section come out of the devised performance *Imaging the Link*, a Mothers by Daughters Project, which took place as part of the Women and Theatre course in Spring 1996 at Loughborough University. The piece was made by a group of seven young women whose work was facilitated by Tanya Myers. My own involvement was rather restricted because I was heavily pregnant with my second child (although the image of the mother-to-be figure making notes on the work in the corner of the drama studio, also, on occasion, became a point of reference in the making processes).

Researching motherhood

As a facilitator, Tanya's ideas for the project were framed by a performance she had made with her own mother and daughter at The Mothers of Invention Symposium, hosted by the Magdalena Project in September 1995. Curiously, but perhaps not surprisingly, the focus on motherhood at this Magdalena Symposium, unlike other events organised by the Project, attracted relatively little interest and only a small number of women took part. The pressure on women to 'appear' to be without children is particularly acute – especially for women working in professional theatre in this country. As Jill Greenhalgh, mother of two daughters and artistic director of The Magdalena Project, stated: 'it almost feels as though we are being treacherous to our work by even giving space to speak about children within an artistic context' (Greenhalgh 1995:1).

The devising group thought about this as an issue in their preliminary discussions and research – particularly as they also had the opportunity to workshop with the director Anna Furse, who talked openly to them about the pressures for women working in theatre to 'pass' as non-mothers.

Part of the group's research also involved looking at motherhood as a problematic area for feminism. Very briefly, we examined and thought about how, in the 1970s, the WLM empowered women to admit to their contradictory feelings about motherhood and to explode the myth of the glorified mother at home with her two-point-four children. Looking at *Top Girls* (see Chapter 7), we talked about how the Tory rhetoric of the 1980s replaced the 1970s feminist de-mystification of the maternal with a new myth of the 'super-career-mum'. Now, in the 1990s we felt it seemed impossible to discuss the difficulties of being a working mother without appearing to join the backlash against feminism: any criticism looks like a nostalgic yearning to be back in the home.

We also thought about some of the objections raised by feminists of earlier mother-and-daughter theatre projects. For example, Jill Dolan describes *The Daughter's Cycle Trilogy* (1977–1980) by the American women's company, The Women's Experimental Theatre (WET), and considers the potential pitfalls of creating a performance that idealises the mother-and-daughter relationship, which figures motherhood as the biologically determined path to a woman's self-fulfilment (Dolan 1988: 86–97). Thinking about Dolan's critique helped to focus on the possibility of the 'mother–daughter relation-ship' not as 'a device for establishing…commonality and smoothing over the differences between women' (*Ibid.*: 91), but for exploring difference and diversity of individual experience within a collective.

Developing the frame

Although the group had not seen Tanya Myers's original project, she gave them access to her notes to help them frame their own ideas. They looked at the kinds of questions, thoughts and ideas that Tanya, her mother and her daughter had shared and had given them a struc-ture created out of three-generational mother/daughter narratives. Or, rather, four, because working through three generations had made visible a fourth: Florence May, Tanya's grandmother, who had committed suicide. Florence May was an absent presence who did more than haunt the performance: she became its focus. In working through mother–daughter relationships, with a real life mother (Pearl) and daughter (Lily) who are not performers (Pearl describes herself as a socialist housewife; Lily as an environmentalist), Tanya's piece made visible real-life mothers and daughters, and ordinary details from their lives.[1] Aside from the practical difficulties of making theatre with our 'real-life' mothers, many of us, myself included, would not have the emotional courage to embark on such an exploration, but there are other ways of making her 'visible' or representable.

Following the frame of Tanya's original project, the seven women decided to work on a mothers by daughters project with their individual narrative strands collaged into a representation that would not speak for all mother and daughter relationships, but would address personal, political and social narratives experienced individually and collectively within their group. To frame the work, they set themselves group tasks. They conducted questionnaires with their mothers, and with themselves as daughters (see the next section on oral history). They also had to go away to find the following materials that they associated with their mothers:

- a personal object
- a story, tale, poem or rhyme
- a song or piece of music
- a dream
- a game or childhood activity
- an image
- a colour
- something you eat
- part of your body
- something you want to say to your mother, but can't.

If you try this kind of project for yourselves, you will, of course, want to think of your own materials to explore. The group could make the list together, making sure that every woman puts forward a suggestion of a resource they would like the group to find. As in any devising project your group has to be prepared to let some of these go. There is never time to work through everything. Moreover, not all of the materials workshopped will necessarily be taken through to a performance showing.

The following sections show some of the ways that the devising group found to take their tasks forward in workshopping practice.

Oral history

Working with oral history is an important feminist strategy for recovering detail about women's lives – the kind of detail that is left out of the history books. Conducting questionnaires with mothers is a way of finding out ordinary details about their lives, ambitions and experiences.

If you try this exercise – and it is a very good way of raising an awareness of individual maternal histories – have a group discussion about the questions you want to ask. Encourage every woman to put forward a question they want to ask. Also be aware that even if you think you can anticipate the response, there will be surprises, although these often yield some of the most fertile material to work with. For example, the group did not set a specific question about work, but it figured repeatedly in the personal histories:

> The most significant thing I can remember is going for a job with very young children and being discriminated against....I was at home when you were little – a dedicated mother. Then I went to work part-time to fit in around you...I have a career now. When you were little I was 100% mum. That was my role.
>
> (Mother of Sam Jevons, devising-performer, 1996)

You may want to use the oral material just as a way of sharing maternal histories at the start of a project. Or, you may want to put some of the oral material directly into your performance, or find ways of physicalising it (see under 'shared objects').

Personal objects

The group adapted Castrillo's personal object exercise to a 'personal object I associate with my mother' exercise. Working privately and eventually sharing the private object work was a way of bringing the 'real life' mother into the frame:

> My personal object was my Mum's cloudy quartz stone as I remember her always wearing this when I was a child. It is also very important to my Mum, as my Dad gave it to her on their wedding day. I was very protective of my object because it is so

precious to us both and because within the rehearsal space it was a physical expression of my Mum's presence.

(Justine Greene, devising-performer, 1996)

Objects could, therefore, function metonymically, standing in for the mother. Bringing them into the space was a way of bringing the 'mother' into the space to begin work. In the performance the personal objects were used as an 'exhibition' between the performance space and the spectators, and performers talked to spectators individually after the performance about their objects and other personal material collected with them, used in the making process, telling the stories behind them. You can use this as a way of encouraging your spectators to begin to share their stories as they respond to the materials on display.

Shared objects

Although the personal objects remained solely with the women (and their mothers) to whom they belonged, there were other objects that the group could work with all together. Food and towels were key shared objects (see also Chapter 8 on 'Everyday objects', p. 148). Food was inspired by watching Bobby Baker's *Drawing on a Mother's Experience* (see the Resources section). Different women in different sessions would take turns to feed the group and tell the story they associated with the food while acting this out. Towels – of the large, soft, bath variety – were used for regular improvisations. They have so many associations: of being hugged, comforted and made safe by mums. But they were also used to image the hard work of mothers: a *Gestus* for showing the mother as the worker, picking up all the towels and drying each 'child' in turn. This was a way of physicalising and imaging detail from the oral histories about the very hard work that goes into a career looking after young children.

Word associations

Very simple word association games were played with key words – most obviously 'mother' and 'daughter':

We played a word association game. One woman would begin with a word associated with the mother–daughter relationship. Women would join in offering a word or sentence relating to the previous word, whenever they felt ready to speak. We found that, sometimes, two or more women would speak simultaneously – especially when we were talking about being comforted, or about having fun times with our mothers. But when the game reached a point where we were talking about our relationships with our mothers now, there would be silences as expressions of guilt or anger emerged.

(Tina Savage, devising-performer, 1996)

If you try this kind of exercise, what you will find is that while there may be points of contact in word associations, using key words such as 'mother' and 'daughter' will reveal a whole range of responses based on individual experience: plurality rather than universality, truths rather than truth. (In Tanya Myers' original project, for example, the first word on Pearl's list of 'mother' associations was suicide).

In performance, the word association game was included as a semi-spontaneous event: the women knew where it was coming in the piece, had a position to take up in the performance space, but would not know beforehand exactly what they would say. They allowed themselves to speak individually and to respond collectively: to try and fragment the myth of mother/daughter universality or commonality.

Family photo-frames

Very simple exercises of using the group to create body sculptures of how they see their families and how they would like to see them generated very strong emotional responses. This is particularly so of the moment when the woman directing her family tableau finally positions herself in the frame of her family as she would like to see it – perhaps because there is someone she would like to take out of the frame, see in it, see differently and so on.

The simplicity of this kind of work belies its emotional content. So if trying out this exercise, your group needs to be aware of, supportive and ready for emotions as they come up. Being part of someone else's frame is a way of sharing the emotions, and a way of collaging individual and group responses.

The women/daughters involved in *Imaging the Link* found that this autobiographical performance work raised their awareness of the social and cultural fabric of their mothers' lives. The oral histories used in the beginning work taught them about the realities of birthing, raising young families, combining childcare with work or juggling motherhood with personhood. Woven together, the individual histories of mothers by daughters made 'visible' a collective narrative of contemporary maternity.

Case study 2: *Self-ish*

The second autobiographical project (Spring 1997) was designed for six devising-performers to explore their childhood and teenage experiences of growing up in the Thatcher years.[2] While they were too young to have had a grasp on the political scene of the 1980s, what emerged overwhelmingly in preliminary discussions was how strongly the six women involved felt that they had been pressured by 'top girl' ideology to succeed educationally, materially and sexually. They had grown up with blonde, material girl, Madonna, as their icon, promising them sexual freedom and economic success. In retrospect, they were aware of the 'gap' between the systems of gender representation that constructed them as 'material girls' and the reality of their 'mis-fit' lives. They wanted to play in this 'gap'; to make a performance about themselves which would use personal histories to engage in the politics of representation. Visually the women signed their refusal to be consumed and fixed as gender stereotypes as they put on, took off and slipped in and out of constructed images of femininity, in a 'this is me, but not me' performance register. The workshopping suggestions that follow are ones that you might wish to try out and to adapt in a 'this-represents-me-but-is-not-me' exploration about yourselves. ('Self-ish' for us was a way of signalling the self as subject and agent of the performance, but also of indexing the capitalist greed of the 'selfish' 1980s.)

Memory props

One way of getting started on this kind of autobiographical project is for members of your group to go away and to find a number of 'props' (possessions) that you can use to workshop personal histories. Again, your group will need to decide what it considers important to bring back to work with, but to give you some ideas, here is a selection from the 'memory props' which the *Self-ish* group decided on:

- items of clothing (past and present);
- childhood toys;

- popular songs (from teenage years);
- children's books and teenage magazines;
- images of female icons;
- family photographs.

Displays

Memories will begin to surface as you go away to hunt through trea-sured belongings and personal memorabilia. When these are brought back to the group, each woman could create a display of her own 'props'/memories. Each woman in turn can take the group through her collection. If you have come up with particular songs, play these back while working through the collection. Again, do not be surprised if unexpected memories arise as you work. Allow for group responses, and also allow time for everyone to browse the displays, to make a note of vivid memories, and to record those memories, narratives or emotions that have surfaced as a shared point of refer-ence in the group.

Making a spectacle of myself: monologues

Try devising your own monologues in response to the heading 'Making a spectacle of myself'. We found that 'spectacle' monologues, which recall an occasion when you presented or 'performed' yourself in a way that went wrong, offered a way of developing personal narratives that highlighted the image-making process. Memories of such occasions tend to be very strong, self-revealing, and may, poten-tially, generate much autobiographical material. Prepared and improvised 'spectacle' monologues were delivered with microphones to create a stand-up-autobiographical register (Claire Dowie style). Amplified voices offer a way of creating a resistant 'gap' between the narrative and the speaker.

Making a 'self'

For exploring a 'this is me, but not me' performance register, try making life-size versions of your selves. We found that working with a fabric 'self' was an excellent prop for 'self-ish' workshopping (see Plates 5 and 6).

What is distinctive about working with your 'self', as opposed, for example, to other ways you might try and foreground the 'doll-like'

Plate 5 Self-ish workshopping

Plate 6 Self-ish workshopping

pressures of femininity for women is that you fashion the 'self' out of your own body, and whatever you add on to your 'self' there will always be patches of white fabric showing; we see the seams and raw edges. The Appendix (pp. 191–4) gives you a step-by-step guide to make your 'self' out of card or out of fabric depending on your time, needs or resources. Here are some suggestions for workshopping your 'selves'.

- Improvise with your 'self' to find out how you 'see' yourself, how you feel about your own body, how you want to hold it, carry it, walk with it and so on (see Plates 5 and 6). These can be quite surprising: 'I was disgusted with the image of myself which appeared shapeless and unfeminine.…While others were more protective of their "selves" (Chrissie brought her self on, carrying it like a baby), I brought mine on by kicking it, because I was angry with the image I'd created' (Emma Healey, devising-performer, 1997).
- Explore your 'self' as a white canvas on which you can add photos, jewellery, clothing or pictures of female icons. Sculpt your 'self' into the display of 'memory' props you started with. Try a group sculpture of 'selves' and possessions.
- A jointed, movable self is one you can play with in relation to posture and movement. Try and re-create your 'self' in some simple everyday situations: 'you' sitting at your desk, 'you' relaxing, 'you' driving, 'you' looking in a mirror. Play your music and see how you want your 'self' to look or to move.
- Work yourself as a puppet to play out different image-making or spectacle-making narratives. Try using some of the 'how-to-be' materials for this (see earlier), and use your 'self' to parody a 'how-to-be' sequence.

Photoboards

Family photographs were used to brainstorm memories of special occasions, feelings about childhood and familial relations, and so on (see earlier). You can use this kind of brainstorming to generate personal narratives for starting monologues, or for working a narrative into an ensemble, shared sequence. In *Self-ish* all of the photographs were collaged into a display that the women used as a way of drawing attention to themselves as the subject of the performance.

Own diaries, books and magazines

When searching through childhood books and teenage magazines, and so on, women also came across their own diaries. As diaries are private records, you may not feel able to work with this material, but if there are extracts that you feel able to make public, you can create resistant commentaries by juxtaposing these with, for example, extracts from teenage romance narratives or childhood fairy stories. You can orchestrate a vocal ensemble for this kind of work, using different voices for different kinds of texts, overlapping them, working a group of voices against a single voice, and so on.

An ending...a beginning

'Fuck you, for thinking any one of these is *me*' was the angry note on which *Self-ish* ended (extracted from Williamson 1983: 102. See Chapter 4, p. 62). The anger was a shared anger of recognition as the devising performers acknowledged their awareness of the systems of gender representation that had oppressed them when growing up, and were continuing to oppress them as young women. When they looked at themselves as the re/source for creating the performance text, these young women found that the politics of representation was what concerned them the most. This brings me to my concluding point: workshopping autobiography may help you to decide on your own political, feminist agenda.

In brief, unless there are a number of mature women students in your group, studying theatre in higher education will generally involve you working with young women whose lives did not coincide with a high point of feminist activity, and this will increasingly be the case for future generations of young women as we move into the twenty-first century. While you can look at the three feminist positions most commonly described as they have been throughout this study as bourgeois, cultural and materialist–feminist, and work out from the surrounding literature that the most desirable of these is materialist feminism, your responses may often be rooted in 'second-hand' readings rather than first-hand experience. Feminism may often feel like something that is outside of rather than inside your lives. However, in researching your own lives, your own experiences, you look at yourself as subject and object in the social, political, theatrical and cultural matrix. What you decide has been oppressive to you, and to the women in your group, you can turn into a resistant, oppositional, angry voice that refuses to be silenced. At the same time as you create a feminist theatre practice based on what is *in* your lives, you are deciding on and defining a future for feminism.

RESOURCES

On feminist theoretical approaches to auto/biography try Stanley (1992) and Swindells (1995).

Bobby Baker's video *Drawing On a Mother's Experience* (1995) is distributed by Artsadmin., London. Dowie's stand-up theatre plays are collected in Dowie (1996).

On mothers and daughters try Joanna Goldsworthy's (ed.) collection *Mothers by Daughters* (London: Virago, 1995), or Carolyn Steedman's autobiographically based study of 'two lives' (her own and her mother's) in *Landscape for a Good Woman* (London: Virago, 1986). For dramatic examples of staging mother and daughter dialogues you might have a look at Marsha Norman's *'night Mother* (New York: Hill and Wang, 1983) or Sharman Macdonald's *When I was a Girl, I used to Scream and Shout* in *Plays 1* (London: Faber, 1995). For an American overview of mother/daughter feminist stage work, see Canning (1996), Chapter 4. See also the dramatic material and resources section in Chapter 7.

For autobiographical collections try the pioneering volume *Dutiful Daughters: Women Talk About Their Lives* edited by Jean McCringle and Sheila Rowbotham (Harmondsworth: Penguin, 1977). Among the Virago collections, you might sample L. Heron (ed.) *Truth, Dare or Promise* (London: Virago, 1985), which examines the lives of young women growing up in the 1950s; S. Maitland (ed.) *Very Heaven* (London: Virago, 1988), which details women's recollections of the 1960s; and J. Scanlon *Surviving the Blues* (London: Virago, 1990), which looks at the lives of young women growing up in the 1980s.

Appendix: to make your 'self'

MATERIALS

1	**Large (woman-sized) pieces of paper**	cut from a roll of newsprint, lining paper or brown wrapping paper. Failing this, newspaper stuck together with masking tape is possible.
2	**Fat felt pens**	for drawing the outline.
3	**Corrugated card**	old cardboard boxes are ideal. Only one layer of corrugation is best. Make sure there is enough length to cut arms and legs without creases.
4	**Sharp scissors or craft knife/scalpel**	
5	**Eight buttons**	about 2 cm in diameter, pierced through with holes.
6	**Fishing twine**	extra strong thread or nylon; wool is not as strong but will do.
7	**Wire**	about the thickness of coat-hanger wire or a little less so that you can bend it by hand.
8	**Wire cutters**	
9	**Gaffa tape**	or other strong thick tape, such as brown parcel tape.
10	**Calico**	or use a similar type of fabric. Old sheets work well if you avoid any worn patches.
11	**Sewing thread**	
12	**Stuffing**	kapok or similar material is best, or foam chips (messy) or cut up wadding or even old tights or soft fabric such as old jerseys cut into squares.

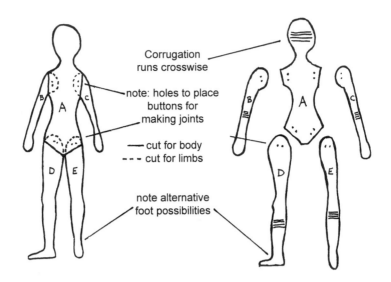

Diagram 1

INSTRUCTIONS

Version I (See Diagrams I and 2)

1　This is easier if you wear something like leggings and a T-shirt and work in pairs. Lie on the paper whilst your partner draws round you, holding the pen upright and getting as close to the sides of your body as possible. Details such as fingers and hair are not important but make sure that your partner draws right up under the arms and between the legs. Feet can be drawn out to the side or missed off altogether.

2　Cut out the outline.

3　Use the outline to make the five pieces of Self from corrugated cardboard: A head and body; B and C arms; D and E legs.

　　Make sure that the corrugation is running across the limbs so that you can get a good bend at elbows and knees. Remember to cut out the overlaps (see Diagram 1) and label left and right limbs.

4   Make a pair of holes through the two layers of card in the four places indicated in Diagram 2, using the points of a pair of scissors or a pair of compasses.

5   Before you do this, decide whether you are going as far as Version 3. If so, do step 7 now.

     To join each limb to the body, take a piece of twine about 30 cm long and then pass it through a button, through a corresponding hole in the body, then through the other button, then back through the other set of holes and tie off fairly tightly. (This is much easier than it sounds! See Diagram 2.)

You now have a useable articulated Self. This may be all you need, have time for, or can afford.

Version 2

Construct shape as Version 1 by following instructions 1– 5 above.

6   Cut a piece of wire a little less than the length of the head/body piece. Tape it to the centre of the card. Do the same on the arms and legs. With a fairly thin card and a fairly thick piece of galvanised wire, this will give you much more flexibility than cardboard alone.

Version 3

7   Follow the instructions for Version 1 as far as step 4. Lay your pieces of card onto a double layer of calico or similar fabric. Draw round them about an inch away from the edge. These

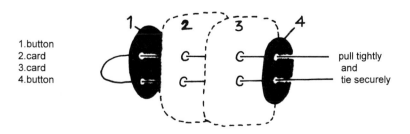

1.button
2.card
3.card
4.button

pull tightly
and
tie securely

Diagram 2

form your sewing lines and will allow enough room for the stuffing. Allow a little more than an inch and also some extra length at the ends of the limbs. Cut the fabric about 1cm outside sewing lines.

8   Join the cardboard body as in Version 1, step 5.

9   Sew the fabric you have cut out to make the limbs leaving an opening at the ends that will be attached to the body. It is much quicker if you use a sewing machine. Turn inside out.

10   Sew the fabric you have cut out for the head and the body. You will probably have to leave one side of the head and neck open, and at least some of one side of the body so that you can achieve step 11. Trim all curves and then turn inside out.

11   Fit the fabric head and body over the cardboard one. Lightly stuff the head and neck on both sides of the card, then pin and sew up by hand. Be careful not to overstuff one side or you won't be able to fit any stuffing in the other. Do the same for the body. There is no need to try and shape breasts or bottom in stuffing. These can be added on later.

12   Pull the pieces of fabric for the arms and legs over the appropriate pieces of cardboard and stuff in the same way as for the head and body. Use a long ruler or a stick to push the stuffing down to the end of the limbs.

13   Pin and sew the limbs to the body, making sure that you allow enough fabric at the joints for them to move: pin the underarms and inside legs with the limbs extended out and upwards; pin the shoulders and outer thighs with the legs together and arms held together on the tummy. Do not worry about the quality of your needlework. It all adds to the character of your 'Self'.

14   Personalise as appropriate. We made breasts and 'saggy bits' from washed, stuffed muslin and sewed them on by hand. We made hair from strips of different colours/textures of material. What you do with yours is up to you.

Glossary

FEMINIST THEORY

bourgeois feminism   also known as **liberal feminism**, designates the least radical of feminist positions. The bourgeois feminist view proposes the amelioration of women's position with the minimum amount of change to the social, political, economic and cultural systems of power already in place. To give an example: the bourgeois feminist would advocate greater numbers of women in parliament, without proposing to change the masculinist structures of government and of governing.

canon (adj. canonical)   a body of work deemed to be 'great'. Canonical texts are those that are culturally 'valued', such as works by Shakespeare, Dickens or Lawrence. Literary or theatrical canons have, therefore, been re-visited by feminist scholarship to highlight the gender-bias of the canon, which reflects male domination of economic, social and cultural systems.

consciousness-raising (CR)   the process of becoming aware of oppression and advocating rights. Women formed discussion groups, CR groups, in the 1970s to talk through their oppression and to raise awareness of inequality.

cultural feminism   also known as **radical feminism** sees the oppression of women in the **patriarchal**, male-dominated systems of power. Cultural feminism looks instead to woman-identified models of social and cultural organisation. More radical than **bourgeois feminism**, it fails, however, to consider issues of class and race pertinent to **materialist feminism**.

cultural sniping   is **Jo Spence**'s concept for describing a need to act as a cultural terrorist; to fight back at dominant culture from which women may find themselves excluded on the basis of gender, class, race or sexuality.

écriture féminine   proposed by French feminist Hélène Cixous (see **French feminist theory**), is the call for 'woman to write herself'; to find her own voice or 'language' out in the margins of the male **symbolic** order. To find her voice she must be re-located in the pre-Oedipal imaginary (see under **Lacan**) and return to the 'body' from which she has been driven away in the realm of the **symbolic**.

French feminist theory   is associated with Hélène Cixous, Luce Irigaray and Julia Kristeva. This is a 'body' of continental theory concerned primarily with women's subjectivity in relation to language and writing. Although diverse in many ways, all three of these theorists draw on a **Lacanian** model of psychoanalysis to arrive at an understanding of women's marginal relation to the **symbolic** organisation of language and communication (see also **écriture féminine**).

gaze   often referred to as the 'male gaze', conceptualises the way in which men look and women are the objects to be looked at. The gaze was pioneered in film studies by Laura Mulvey and although the term has since been subjected to more complex theorising, remains useful for understanding en-gendered modes of looking, especially in visual art forms.

heteropatriarchy (adj. heteropatriarchal)   refers to the dominance of heterosexuality and **patriarchy** in our organisation of sexual and social systems; the marginalisation of same-sex relations and of women.

Lacan, Jacques (adj. Lacanian)   re-framed Freud to look at how subjectivity is constructed through language. Briefly, in a Lacanian model the point at which a child enters language is metaphorically represented as the 'mirror stage'. Entry into language means the entry into an external order that constructs the child's identity. Psychosexually, this is the moment in which the pre-Oedipal/imaginary link with the Mother is severed, in favour of the **symbolic**/Father. This model has been re-worked by feminists (see under **French feminist theory**) to explore women's subjectivity and marginalisation in relation to the arbitrarily imposed symbolic order.

liberal feminism   see **bourgeois feminism**.

logocentrism (adj. logocentric)   is the privileging of *Logos*, 'the Word', in Western thinking, where the Word is understood to operate as a **symbolic**, controlling **patriarchal** system in collusion with **phallocentrism**. It is a central tenet in the philosophy of Cixous (see under **French feminist theory**).

masquerade (of femininity)   is a concept to describe the ways in which women might protest against their alienation or marginalisation in the **symbolic** realm of the masculine by miming the masquerade of femininity imposed on them. Theoretically, the concept of miming the mime imposed on women is explored in the work of Luce Irigaray (see under **French feminist theory**).

materialist feminism   also known as **socialist feminism** locates the oppression of women in the historical and material conditions of class, race and gender. Unlike **bourgeois feminism**, it demands the radical transformation of social, cultural and economic systems of power in the interests of a more equal society.

patriarchy (adj. patriarchal)   a society dominated by men. **Cultural feminism** sees the patriarchal organisation of society as a primary cause of women's oppression.

performativity   a concept based on speech–act theory, and re-worked by feminist theorists such as Judith Butler to explain how identities are constructed through frequentative and complex citational processes that negate the possibility of the freedom to 'choose' gender.

Personal is Political   the slogan of the 1970s Women's Liberation Movement, which encouraged women to view their domestic lives as a political issue.

phallocentrism (adj. phallocentric)   the male-centred privileging of the phallus as a sign of male power.

queer   a term originally used to refer to homosexuals, now reappropriated in queer theory and politics to refute the seemingly 'natural' formations of gender and heterosexuality as the 'norm'.

radical feminism   see **cultural feminism**.

resisting reader   Judith Fetterley's concept for the feminist reader who has to resist the ideological work of texts from which she finds herself excluded on gender grounds.

semiotic   see **symbolic**.

symbolic   derived from the Lacanian opposition between the
imaginary and the symbolic, the term symbolic has been
widely adopted by feminists to refer to our dominant systems
of communicating and writing as male or **patriarchal**.
Kristeva (see under **French feminist theory**) replaced 'the
imaginary and the symbolic' with 'semiotic and the symbolic'.
In this psychoanalytic framing, those subjects on the margins
of society, like women, will be driven towards the semiotic in
the desire to escape alienation and oppression in the symbolic.

PRACTITIONERS

This section includes women playwrights, practitioners and gender-
aware companies cited in the volume.

Adams, Gilly   Drama Officer until 1981 at the Welsh Arts Council
and former artistic director of the Made in Wales Stage
Company. Now freelance and organising workshops for the
Magdalena Project.

Aniksdal, Geddy   a performer and director with Grenland
Friteater, Norway. Aniksdal performs and workshops regularly
with the **Magdalena Project**, using her physical skills to
encourage creativity, writing and performance in other
women.

Armstrong, Frankie   began singing skiffle in the late 1950s and
joined the folk scene. Armstrong's feminist voice work is
influenced by her research into traditional women's songs and
singing. She workshops and performs internationally
encouraging singers and non-singers to free up their voices.

Baker, Bobby   a performance artist who trained as a painter and
began performance work by 'painting' with food. Baker's
performances, in particular *Drawing on a Mother's Experience*,
politicise the ordinary detail of women's domestic lives. In
1991 she created *Kitchen Show*, opening up her own London
kitchen as the performance venue. Baker's work is available on
video from her Daily Life Company at Arts admin. London.

Baker, Elizabeth   a turn-of-the-century dramatist best known for
her play *Chains* (1909). Baker went on to have an extensive
playwriting career, most notably at Birmingham Repertory
Theatre during the 1920s. She was primarily concerned with

the dramatisation of women struggling to carve out lives for themselves other than in domestic drudgery and marriage.

Behn, Aphra a seventeenth-century woman writer, reputedly the first woman playwright to earn an independent living writing for theatre. Behn's work had largely disappeared from the theatrical **canon**, until feminist research recovered it.

Bell, Florence a close friend of **Elizabeth Robins**, with whom she collaborated on *Alan's Wife*. Bell's own work includes a range of playwriting, essays and fiction. She is most particularly remembered for her publication of *At the Work: A Study of a Manufacturing Town* (1907).

Benmussa, Simone a French feminist director whose productions at the New End Theatre, London of *The Singular Life of Albert Nobbs* (1978) and *Portrait of Dora* (1979), brought her critical acclaim in the UK. Subsequently, these two plays have been of particular interest to feminist theatre scholarship: *The Singular Life* on account of its principal cross-dressing device and *Dora* for its revisioning of Freud.

Bron, Eleanor an actress and writer whose performance work has ranged from satirical cabaret in the 1960s, to the playing of classical stage roles, including Hedda Gabler and the Duchess of Malfi. Bron has numerous film (e.g. Ken Russell's *Women in Love*) and television credits.

Castrillo, Cristina an Argentinian director and co-founder of the Latin American theatre company, Libre Teatro Libre, in 1969. In 1980 Castrillo founded Teatro Delle Radici in Lugano, Switzerland, where she trains her own company. Castrillo places an emphasis on the performer as the creator of her own performance, working through physical and emotional memories of the body and of personal histories.

Chadwick, Helen a voice specialist who frequently gives voice workshops for the Magdalena Project. In addition to her workshops, and voice coaching at the National Theatre, Chadwick creates her own performances and vocal recordings.

Chapman, Clair see **Spare Tyre**.

Chowdhry, Maya an Asian playwright who works on themes of identity, race and sexuality. Chowdhry's *Monsoon*, published in Kadija George (ed.) *Black and Asian Women Writers* (London: Aurora Metro, 1993) explores the taboo subject of women's menstruation, and sexuality.

Churchill, Caryl   a leading, international, contemporary British
   playwright. Churchill's work spans a range of socialist and
   feminist issues (see Chapter 7). In recent years her work has
   become increasingly experimental in style, most especially in
   productions where she works with the physical company,
   Second Stride, who performed *The Skriker* (1994, see
   Kathryn Hunter) and *Hotel* (1997).
Cusack, Sinead   comes from the Cusack theatre family. She has
   had an extensive career in the RSC and has tackled a range of
   Shakespearean roles from both the tragedies and the
   comedies.
Daniels, Sarah   a playwright known for her biting humour and
   foregrounding of lesbian characters. Savaged by male critics
   for *Masterpieces* (1983), her play about pornography, Daniels
   continues to tackle social issues, particularly women's mental
   health and child abuse: *Beside Herself* (1990), *Head-Rot Holiday*
   (1992), and *The Madness of Esme and Shaz* (1994).
de Angelis, April   a former actress turned playwright whose work
   has been performed at the Royal Court, and by companies
   which include **Paines Plough** and **The Sphinx**. She has
   written issue-based woman-centred plays, but is more
   particularly recognised for her experimental approaches to
   dramatic form.
Dorothy Talk   a theatre company founded by ex-**Siren** members
   Jude Winter and **Hilary Ramsden**. The company's work
   has combined a physical style of performance with an interest
   in sexual politics, most significantly in their 1992 cross-dressed
   production of *Walking on Peas*, by Erika Block.
Dowie, Claire   an anarchic writer and performer of stand-up
   theatre plays that tackle sexual politics and sexual identities.
   Her stand-up play *Why is John Lennon Wearing a Skirt?* was
   winner of the London fringe award in 1991.
DV8 Physical Theatre   was formed in 1986 with the production
   My Sex, Our Dance, to challenge traditional approaches to
   dance and to foreground sexual politics in company work.
   Risk-taking productions have included *Dead Dreams of
   Monochrome Men* (1988) based on the life of the serial killer
   Dennis Nilson, and *Enter Achilles* (1996), which explores the
   'strait-jacket of masculinity'.
Fascinating Aïda   a cabaret trio popular in the 1980s who used a
   style of over-glamorised femininity to satirise the 1980s

'Superwoman' ethos. Their songs were a mixture of ridiculous, camp numbers such as 'Sew on a Sequin', and left-wing laments, as in 'Socialist Britain'.

Fairbanks, Tasha see **Siren**.

Foursight Theatre a women's company founded in 1987 who specialise in devising theatre based on women's biography. The group had particular success with *Bloody Mary and the Virgin Queen* (1993), devised by the company.

Furse, Anna a director and former artistic director of the new writing company **Paines Plough**. Furse has been internationally acclaimed for her writing and direction of *Augustine (Big Hysteria)* (1991), and took part in the BBC television series *Making Babies* (1996), profiling women and IVF treatment.

Gay Sweatshop a gay touring theatre company founded in 1975 by Drew Griffiths and Gerald Chapman. Over the years the company has given support to new work by gay writers, and has survived several funding crises. **Lois Weaver** of **Split Britches** was appointed co-artistic director of the company in 1992, where she stayed for four years, nurturing solo **queer** performances and queer school training.

Gems, Pam a working-class woman playwright whose long career in the theatre was established in the feminist fringe of the 1970s, since when she has had a long association with the RSC and more recently is one of a handful of women writers to be staged at the National. She is best known for her biographical plays such as *Queen Christina* (RSC, 1997), *Piaf* (RSC, 1978), and, more recently, *Marlene* (Oldham, 1996) and *Stanley* (RNT, 1996).

Greenhlagh, Jill artistic director of the Magdalena Project.

Hanna, Gillian see **Monstrous Regiment**.

Hunter, Kathryn a founding member of the experimental, physical theatre company Théâtre de Complicité (UK). Her many acting credits include Lear in **Kaut-Howson**'s Leicester production and the title role in **Caryl Churchill**'s *The Skriker*.

It's All Right to be Woman Theatre a US women's company formed in 1970, who used **CR** methods to turn women's experiences into woman-centred performances. Performing to all-women's audiences, the group work typified a **cultural (radical) feminist** approach to theatre-making.

Joint Stock   a fringe company founded in 1974 by William Gaskill and Max Stafford-Clark. Joint Stock were known during their time as a company who specialised in collaborative ensemble playing, using relatively long periods of research and workshopping in production work. In 1993 Stafford-Clark formed the touring company Out of Joint.

Kalinska, Zofia   a Polish director and performer who worked with Tadeusz Kantor. In 1984 she founded Poland's first all-women's company, Akne Theatre. Kalinska has strong links with the **Magdalena Project** and with Meeting Ground (see **Tanya Myers**). She works centrally on female archetypes and has developed her own solo performance on the figure of Medea.

Kaut-Howson, Helena   a Polish-born director whose work has been staged internationally in Britain, Poland, Israel, Ireland and Canada. Her professional directing of Shakespeare includes *All's Well That Ends Well*, *Macbeth* and, with **Kathryn Hunter** in the title role, *King Lear*.

Keatley, Charlotte   a contemporary British woman playwright best known for her play *My Mother Said I Never Should* (see Chapter 7, this volume). Keatley's other theatre work includes *Dressing for Dinner*, written for the three-woman company, Royale Ballé, which she set up in 1984, and plays for children.

Lavery, Bryony   a lesbian playwright whose prolific output includes plays for Clean Break, **Gay Sweatshop**, **Monstrous Regiment** and the **Women's Theatre Group**. Her playwriting is particularly noted for its sexual politics, stylistic range and comic strength.

Luckham, Claire   a playwright best known for *Trafford Tanzi* (1978), her comedy on sexual politics which is staged in a wrestling ring. Luckham has continued to write woman-centred plays, including *The Choice* (1992), a play about Down's syndrome. *Scum* was co-scripted with her husband Chris Bond, then director of Liverpool's Everyman theatre.

Magdalena Project   the International Network of Women in Contemporary Theatre, founded in 1986. The Project organises international symposiums, workshops and performances with a focus on women's theatre practice, and houses an archive of women and performance material at Cardiff (UK).

McCusker, Mary   see **Monstrous Regiment**.

Monstrous Regiment   a socialist–feminist theatre company founded in 1975 by Gillian Hanna, Mary McCusker and Chris Bowler. The company commissioned and performed new work by British and European women playwrights until 1993, when lack of funds forced them to cease touring.

Mrs Worthington's Daughters   a feminist company founded in 1978 with a commitment to recovering plays by or about women from the past. Founding member Julie Holledge published a study of women in Edwardian theatre, *Innocent Flowers* (London: Virago, 1981).

Myers, Tanya   a performer and founding member of the Meeting Ground Theatre Company, based in Nottingham (UK). Meeting Ground specialises in international, collaborative projects, particularly with the former East European block, and works extensively with the Polish director **Zofia Kalinska**.

Paines Plough   a new writing theatre company established in 1975. The company is not specifically a women's company but under the administration of **Anna Furse** in the early 1990s, it supported women through writers' salons. See also **April de Angelis**.

Rame, Franca   an Italian actress and playwright who performs her own hard-hitting feminist monologues, which tackle issues such as rape and the isolation of women in the home. With her playwright husband Dario Fo, she is known for her political and satirical style of work. Four of her monologues were translated by Gillian Hanna and performed by **Monstrous Regiment** in 1983.

Ramsden, Hilary   a physically trained performer who joined **Siren** and subsequently co-founded **Dorothy Talk** with **Jude Winter**.

Red Ladder   a socialist and feminist company with a long history of socialist productions in the 1970s. Their first 'women's play', *Strike While the Iron is Hot*, was performed in 1972. The company has transformed over the years into a multi-racial touring company that performs primarily to young audiences with shows designed to raise social and political awareness. Shows are accompanied by discussions and workshops.

Robins, Elizabeth   was born in America, but spent much of her career performing and writing in England. She was acclaimed as a 'new' actress in Edwardian theatre, and was the first woman to play Hedda Gabler on the British stage. Her suffrage play *Votes for Women* was performed at the Court Theatre in 1907.

Shaw, Fiona   an actress who has played a range of Shakespearean roles for the RSC. Her many other acting credits include the award-winning performance of Electra, also for the RSC. Shaw often works closely with the director **Deborah Warner** and had the solo role in Warner's banned Beckett revival of *Footfalls*.

Sherman, Cindy   a New York-based photographer whose work attracts the interest of feminists on account of her representations of femininity. Sherman's early work is of particular relevance to **masquerade**: she photographs herself as a feminine construct with the purpose of drawing the spectator's attention to the imposition of feminine identities on women. In particular, her black and white photography, evocative of Hitchcock-style movie stills, pushes the construct of femininity towards the grotesque.

Siren   a UK lesbian theatre company founded in 1979 by **Jude Winter**, Tasha Fairbanks and Jane Boston. Until 1989, when the company folded, Siren was the foremost company in England for lesbian performance.

Sklar, Roberta   a founding member of the American Women's Experimental Theater company in the 1970s; see under **WET**.

Sowerby, Gita   a writer of children's literature and dramatist critically acclaimed for *Rutherford and Son* (1912). *Rutherford* was rediscovered by **Mrs Worthington's Daughters** in 1980, and revived again in 1994 at the National Theatre (the Cottesloe), in a production directed by Katie Mitchell.

Spare Tyre   a company founded in 1979 by Clair Chapman, Katina Noble and Harriet Powell. The group's first production, *Baring the Weight* was inspired by Susie Orbach's *Fat is a Feminist Issue*. The company went on to specialise in productions that focused on women's bodies, sexuality and relations, working predominantly through a play-with-music form.

Sphinx   see under **Women's Theatre Group**.

Spence, Jo   a feminist photographer whose pioneering range of work focused on representations of class and gender, in which Spence involved herself as subject. She explored photography as therapy for working through personal, familial and social issues, and visually documented her own fight against cancer. She died in 1992.

Split Britches   is an American theatre company run by Lois Weaver, Peggy Shaw and Deborah Margolin. Since their inaugural production in 1981, which gave the company its name, Split Britches has been responsible for some of the most outstanding lesbian performance work on the international stage.

Suzman, Janet   is an actress who has played a range of classical roles that include Hedda Gabler, Clytaemenestra and the eponymous heroine in Gorky's *Vassa*, under the direction of **Helena Kaut-Howson**.

Wandor, Michelene   is a socialist–feminist writer, playwright, poet and critic. In addition to her own work for theatre and radio, Wandor has given substantial support to feminist theatre: extensively reviewing productions for magazines such as *Time-Out* and *Spare Rib*, and editing the first four volumes of *Plays by Women* in the Methuen series.

Warner, Deborah   is a director who trained in stage management, formed her own fringe company, Kick Theatre, and went on to became director in residence at the RSC, following her RSC directing debut of *Titus Andronicus*, 1987. She moved to the National Theatre in 1990. She works extensively with the actress **Fiona Shaw**, whom she directed in the cross-gendered title role of *Richard II* in the 1995 Cottesloe production, subsequently screened for BBC television (1997).

Weaver, Lois   is a founding member of **Split Britches**. Has worked as co-artistic director of **Gay Sweatshop** in the 1990s and continues to work internationally making her own solo **queer** performances, and to collaborate with her partner Peggy Shaw, also of **Split Britches**.

WET   an American women's company formed in the 1970s by Clare Coss, Sondra Segal and **Roberta Sklar**. The group's first work, *The Daughters Cycle*, was a trilogy of plays focusing on women's roles in the family. Like **Spare Tyre**, the company went on to work on women's relationship to food, making a second trilogy in the early 1980s: *Woman's Body and Other Natural Resources*.

Winter, Jude   is a founding member of the UK lesbian theatre company **Siren** and, subsequently, co-founder of **Dorothy Talk** (1989).

Women's Theatre Group   was formed in the mid-1970s as a women-only company committed to new writing by women. Over the years the company introduced policies that discriminated in favour of work by Black and lesbian women. The company now operates under the name of The Sphinx.

Notes

3 Finding a body, finding a voice

1 Anna Furse used this exercise as part of her warm-up routine to her session on 'writing' signs on the body, see Chapter 4.

4 Enter gender

1 The 'highlight' of the performances given by Charcot's female hysterics at his public lectures was the three-phase seizure known as the *grand hystérie*. Showalter explains the three phases as: the epileptoid phase (the patient lost consciousness and foamed at the mouth); the phase of clownism (the patient produced incredible contortions, distortions of the body), and the phase of *attitudes passionnelles* in which the patient mimed events and emotions from her life (Showalter 1987 [1985]: 150).

2 This work might well be taken up in workshops leading to a production of *Dora*. My concern here, however, is to describe a session that was designed as an end in itself, in order to provide a working example of how you can combine feminist theory with physical playing to refigure a 'father' text.

7 Activating the feminist script

1 The context in which I have talked to young women about their experiences of working on this play, is during interviews for places to study drama on higher degree programmes. After *My Mother* became a set text in English secondary schools, young women tended to single this out as the play they wished to discuss during their interviews.

8 Creating texts

1 There are a number of variants you can try for this kind of playing: working with the group split in two so that half the group works together to look after the object and the other half try to take it from them; or one person has to seek the object, which the others pass to

each other, trying to keep it from her; or two women partner each other to try and keep the object, and so on.

2 The workshopped presentation took place in the Spring of 1995 at Loughborough University as part of the Women and Theatre course.

9 Re-figuring lives

1 This was a feminist workshop presentation devised by three postgraduate women students on the MA programme Theatre and the Representation of Gender. Originally presented at Loughborough University in the Spring term of 1996, the presentation was subsequently adapted for a performance-lecture at the University of Glasgow's Susan Glaspell Conference, May 1996.

2 *Portraits of Rossetti* had two public performances at Loughborough University on 1 December 1994. It was devised and performed by six women undergraduate students taking the course in Women and Theatre. A longer account of this project and the pedagogic context which framed it was published in *Studies in Theatre Production* (see Aston 1995b).

10 Performing your selves

1 E.A. Kaplan's discussion of representations of motherhood examines three main representational spheres: the historical, the psychoanalytical and the fictional, and proposes that a fourth sphere, the 'real life' mother, lies outside the remit of her study, 'because' as Kaplan explains, 'she is not-representable as such' (Kaplan 1992: 6–7) I have since thought that the kind of mother/daughter theatre work discussed here offers a way of bringing Kaplan's fourth, real-life mother into the frame of representation.

2 *Self-ish* was devised in the Spring of 1997 on the undergraduate Gender and Devising course, Loughborough University.

Bibliography

Allain, P. (1994) 'Movement directing', *Total Theatre*, 6 (4): 9.

Armstrong, F. (1975) 'Interview', *Spare Rib*, 33: 43–5.

—— (1985) 'Finding our voices' in N. Jackowska (ed.) *Voices From Arts for Labour*, London and Sydney: Pluto Press, pp. 20–9.

Aston, E. (1995a) *An Introduction to Feminism and Theatre*, London and New York: Routledge.

—— (1995b) '*Portraits of Rossetti:* feminist theory and performance', *Studies in Theatre Production*, 11: 12–23.

—— (ed.) (1997) *Feminist Theatre Voices*, Loughborough: Loughborough Theatre Texts.

Aughterson, K. (ed.) (1995) *Renaissance Woman: Constructions of Femininity in England*, London and New York: Routledge.

Austin, G. (1990) *Feminist Theories for Dramatic Criticism*, Ann Arbor: University of Michigan Press.

—— (1993) '*Resisting the Birth Mark*: subverting Hawthorne in a feminist theory play', in E. Donkin and S. Clement (eds) *Upstaging Big Daddy*, Ann Arbor: University of Michigan Press, pp. 121–32.

Barker, C. (1977) *Theatre Games: A New Approach to Drama Training*, London: Methuen.

Barr, P. (1970) *A Curious Life for a Lady*, London: Secker & Warburg.

Bassnett, S. (1989) *Magdalena: International Women's Experimental Theatre*, Oxford, New York and Munich: Berg.

Belsey, C. (1980) *Critical Practice*, London and New York: Methuen.

Benmussa, S. (1979) 'Introduction', *Benmussa Directs*, London: John Calder.

Boal, A. (1979) *Theater of the Oppressed*, trans. C.A. McBride and M.O.L. McBride, London: Pluto.

—— (1992) *Games for Actors and Non-Actors*, trans. A. Jackson, London and New York: Routledge.

Bourne, B., Shaw, P., Shaw, P. and Weaver, L. (1996) *Belle Reprieve* in S.E. Case (ed.) *Split Britches*, London and New York: Routledge, pp. 49–183.

Brandes, D. and Phillips, H. (1977) *Gamesters' Handbook*, London: Hutchinson.

Bratton, J.S. (1994) 'Working in the margin: women in theatre history', *New Theatre Quarterly*, 38: 122–31.

Bron, E. (1992) 'Forward', in C. Brückner *Desdemona – If You Had Only Spoken!*, London: Virago, pp. vii–xxiv.

Brückner, C. (1992 [1983]) *Desdemona – If You Had Only Spoken!*, trans. Eleanor Bron, London: Virago.

Burk, J.T. (1993) '*Top Girls* and the politics of representation', in E. Donkin and S. Clement (eds) *Upstaging Big Daddy*, Ann Arbor: University of Michigan Press, pp. 67–78.

Butler, J. (1990) *Gender Trouble: Feminism and the Subversion of Identity*, London and New York: Routledge.

—— (1993) *Bodies that Matter: On the Discursive Limits of Sex*, London and New York: Routledge.

Canning, C. (1996) *Feminist Theaters in the U.S.A.*, London and New York: Routledge.

Caplan, B. (1991) 'Zofia Kalinska and the demonic woman: work in progress', in C. Robson (ed.) *Seven Plays by Women: Female Voices, Fighting Lives*, London: Aurora Metro, pp. 15–18.

Carlson, S. (1988) 'Process and product: contemporary British Theatre and its communities of women', *Theatre Research International*, 13 (3): 249–62.

Case, S.-E. (1988) *Feminism and Theatre*, London: Macmillan.

—— (ed.) (1996) *Split Britches: Lesbian Practice / Feminist Performance*, London and New York: Routledge.

Churchill, C. (1982) ' "Afterword" to *Vinegar Tom*', in M. Wandor (ed.) *Plays by Women: Volume One*, London: Methuen, pp. 39–40.

—— (1990 [1982]) *Top Girls* in *Plays: Two*, London: Methuen.

—— (1991) *Top Girls*, student edn, London: Methuen.

Cima, G.G. (1993) 'Strategies for subverting the canon', in E. Donkin and S. Clement (eds) *Upstaging Big Daddy*, Ann Arbor: University of Michigan Press, pp. 91–105.

Cirla, B. (ed.) (1994) 'The voice in theatre', *Magdalena Newsletter*, no. 14.

Cixous, H. (1979) *Portrait of Dora*, in *Benmussa Directs*, London: John Calder, pp. 28–67.

—— (1981 [1975]) 'The laugh of the Medusa', trans. K. Cohen and P. Cohen, in E. Marks and I. de Courtivron (eds) *New French Feminisms*, Brighton: Harvester Press, pp. 245–64.

—— (1984) 'Aller à la mer', trans. B. Kerslake, *Modern Drama*, 4: 546–8.

Clune, J. (1992) 'Lessons in bad behaviour: or how the vote was won', *Studies in Theatre Production*, (5): 4–24.

Daniels, S. (1984) 'There are fifty two per cent of us', *Drama*, 152: 23–4.

—— (1991) *Plays 1: Ripen Our Darkness, The Devil's Gateway, Masterpieces, Neaptide and Byrthrite*, London: Methuen.

——(1994) *Plays 2: The Gut Girls, Beside Herself, Head-Rot Holiday and The Madness of Esme and Shaz*, London: Methuen, 1994.

Davis, T. and Goodall, P. (1987) 'Personally and politically: feminist art practice', in R. Parker and G. Pollock (eds) *Framing Feminism: Art and the Women's Movement: 1970–1985*, London: Pandora, pp. 293–302.

de Angelis, A. and Furse, A. (1991) 'The salon at Paines Plough', in C. Robson (ed.) *Seven Plays By Women: Female Voices, Fighting Lives*, London: Aurora Metro, pp. 26–8.

de Lauretis (1984) *Alice Doesn't: Feminism, Semiotics, Cinema*, Bloomington: Indiana University Press.

—— (1987) *Technologies of Gender: Essays on Theory, Film, and Fiction*, Bloomington: Indiana University Press.

Diamond, E. (1989a) 'Benmussa's adaptations: unauthorized texts from elsewhere', in E. Brater (ed.) *Feminine Focus*, Oxford: Oxford University Press, pp. 64–78.

—— (1989b) 'Mimesis, mimicry and the "true–real"', *Modern Drama*, 32: 58–72.

—— (1989c) '(In)Visible bodies in Churchill's theater', in L. Hart (ed.) *Making a Spectacle*, Anne Arbor: University of Michigan Press, pp. 259–81.

—— (1997) *Unmaking Mimesis*, London and New York: Routledge.

Doane, M. A. (1992 [1982]) 'Film and the masquerade: theorizing the female spectator', in *The Sexual Subject: A Screen Reader in Sexuality*, London and New York: Routledge, pp. 227–43.

Dolan, J. (1988) *The Feminist Spectator as Critic*, Ann Arbor: University of Michigan Press.

Dollimore, J. and Sinfield, A. (eds) (1985) *Political Shakespeare: New Essays in Cultural Materialism*, Manchester: Manchester University Press.

Donkin, E. (1993) 'Black text, white director: issues of race and gender in directing African–American drama', in E. Donkin and S. Clement (eds) *Upstaging Big Daddy*, Ann Arbor: University of Michigan Press, pp. 79–87.

Donkin, E. and Clement, S. (eds) (1993) *Upstaging Big Daddy*, Ann Arbor: University of Michigan Press.

Dowie, C. (1996) *Why is John Lennon Wearing a Skirt? and Other Stand-Up Plays*, London: Methuen.

Feinstein, E. and the Women's Theatre Group (1991) *Lear's Daughters*, in E. Aston and G. Griffin (eds) *Herstory: Plays By Women For Women: Volume 1*, Sheffield: Sheffield Academic Press, pp. 19–69.

Fetterly, J. (1978) *The Resisting Reader: A Feminist Approach to American Fiction*, Bloomington: Indiana University Press.

Fisher, B. (1994) 'Feminist acts: women, pedagogy and theatre of the oppressed', in M. Schutzman and J. Cohen-Cruz (eds) *Playing Boal: Theatre, Therapy, Activism*, London and New York: Routledge, pp. 185–97.

Fitzsimmons, L. (1989) (compiler) *File On Churchill*, London: Methuen.

Fitzsimmons, L. and Gardner, V. (eds) (1991) *New Woman Plays*, London: Methuen.

Forte, J. and Sumption, C. (1993) 'Encountering *Dora*: putting theory into practice', in E. Donkin and S. Clement (eds) *Upstaging Big Daddy*, Ann Arbor: University of Michigan Press, pp. 37–52.

Franey, R. (1973) 'Women in the workshop', *Plays and Players*, November, 24–7.

Freud, S. (1977) *Pelican Freud Library: Volume 8: Case Histories 1: 'Dora' and 'Little Hans'*, Harmondsworth: Penguin.

Furse, A. (1997) *Augustine (Big Hysteria)*, Amsterdam: Harwood Academic Publishers.

Gardner, V. (ed.) (1985) *Sketches from the Actresses' Franchise League*, Nottingham: Nottingham Drama Texts.

Gay, P. (1994) *As She Likes It: Shakespeare's Unruly Women*, London and New York: Routledge.

Goffman, E. (1987 [1976]) *Gender Advertisements*, New York: Harper & Row.

Goodman, L. (1993) *Contemporary Feminist Theatres: To Each Her Own*, London and New York: Routledge.

—— (1996) 'Feminisms and theatres: canon fodder and cultural change', in P. Campbell (ed.) *Analysing Performance*, Manchester: Manchester University Press, pp. 19–42.

Greenhalgh, J. (1992) 'The Magdalena Project', *Women and Theatre Occasional Papers*, 1: 107–10.

—— (1995) 'Motherhood and theatre', *Magdalena Newsletter*, 17: 1.

Hall, K.F. (1995) 'Uses for a dead White male: Shakespeare, feminism, and diversity', *New Theatre Quarterly*, (41): 55–61.

Hamilton, S. (1993) 'Split britches and the *Alcestis* lesson: "What is this Albatross?" ', in E. Donkin and S. Clement (eds) *Upstaging Big Daddy*, Ann Arbor: University of Michigan Press, pp. 133–49.

Hanna, G. (1978) *Feminism and Theatre*, Theatre papers, 2nd series, no. 8, Dartington, Devon: Dartington College.

—— (ed.) (1991) *Monstrous Regiment: Four Plays and a Collective Celebration*, London: Nick Hern.

Harris, G. (1994) 'Gender and devising: *Europe After the Rain (no man's land)*', *Studies in Theatre Production*, (9): 5–15.

Helms, L. (1994) 'Acts of resistance: the feminist player' in D.C. Callaghan, L. Helms and J. Singh, *The Weyward Sisters*, Oxford and Cambridge, Massachusetts: Blackwell.

hooks, bell (1984) *Feminist Theory: From Margin to Center*, Boston: South End Press.

Isaak, J.A. (1996) *Feminism and Contemporary Art*, London and New York: Routledge.

Jardine, L. (1983) *Still Harping on Daughters: Women and Drama in the Age of Shakespeare*, London: Harvester Wheatsheaf.

Kaplan, E.A. (1992) *Motherhood and Representation: The Mother In Popular Culture and Meldorama*, London and New York: Routledge.

Keatley, C. (1990a [1988]) *My Mother Said I Never Should*, revised edn, London: Methuen.

—— (1990b) 'Art form or platform? On women and playwriting', interview, in *New Theatre Quarterly*, 22 (6): 128–40.

—— (1997) 'Interview', in H. Stephenson and N. Langridge (eds) *Rage and Reason:Women Playwrights on Playwriting*, London: Methuen, pp. 71–80.

Knapp, C. (1997) 'Designing for devised performance', *Studies in Theatre Production*, 15: 51–60.

Kristeva, J. (1982 [1979]) 'Women's time', in N.O. Keohane, M.Z. Rosaldo and B.C. Gelpi (eds) *Feminist Theory: A Critique of Ideology*, Brighton: Harvester Press, pp. 31–53.

Love, L. (1995) 'Resisting the "organic": a feminist actor's approach', in P.B. Zarrilli (ed.) *Acting (Re) Considered: Theories and Practices*, London and New York: Routledge, pp. 275–88.

Luckhurst, M. (1996) 'The disembodied voice and theatres of movement', *Women and Theatre Occasional Papers*, 3: 174–89.

Lutterbie, J. (1993) 'Codirecting: a model for men directing feminist plays', in E. Donkin and S. Clement (eds) *Upstaging Big Daddy*, Ann Arbor: University of Michigan Press, pp. 263–76.

MacDonald, C. (1995) 'Assumed identities: feminism, autobiography and performance art', in J. Swindells (ed.) (1995) *The Uses of Autobiography*, London:Taylor & Francis, pp. 187–95.

McLuskie, K. (1985) 'The patriarchal bard: feminist criticsm and Shakespeare: *King Lear* and *Measure for Measure*', in J. Dollimore and A. Sinfield (eds) *Political Shakespeare: New Essays in Cultural Materialism*, Manchester: Manchester University Press, pp. 88–108.

Marsh, J. (1985) *Pre-Raphaelite Sisterhood*, London: Quartet.

Michaels, W. and Sawyer, W. (1993) *A Workshop Approach to Top Girls and Insignificance*, Rozelle: St Clair Press.

Moi, T. (1985) *Sexual/Textual Politics: Feminist Literary Theory*, London: Methuen.

Monstrous Regiment (1997) 'Interview', in E. Aston (ed.) *Feminist Theatre Voices*, Loughborough: Loughborough Theatre Texts, pp. 52–76.

Mulvey, L. (1989) *Visual and Other Pleasures*, Houndmills, Basingstoke, Hampshire and London: Macmillan.

—— (1992 [1975]) 'Visual pleasure and narrative cinema', in *Screen*, pp. 22–34.

Murray, J.H. (ed.) (1982) *Strong-Minded Women: And Other Lost Voices From 19th-Century England*, Harmondsworth: Penguin.

Nava, M. (1980) 'Introduction to *My Mother Says I never Should*', in M. Wandor (ed.) *Strike While the Iron is Hot*, London: Journeyman Press, pp. 115–17.

Oddey, A. (1994) *Devising Theatre: A Practical and Theoretical Handbook*, London and New York: Routledge.

Orbach, S. (1988 [1978]) *Fat is a Feminist Issue*, London: Arrow.

O'Sullivan, S. (1982) 'Passionate beginnings: ideological politics 1969–1972', *Feminist Review*, (11): 70–86.

Personal Narratives Goup (eds) (1989) *Interpreting Women's Lives: Feminist Theory and Personal Narratives*, Bloomington and Indianapolis: Indiana University Press.

Pollock, G. (1992 [1977]) 'What's wrong with "images of women"?' in *The Sexual Subject: A Screen Reader in Sexuality*, London and New York: Routledge, pp. 135–45.

Poulter, C. (1987) *Playing the Game*, Houndmills, Basingstoke, Hampshire and London: Macmillan.

Ramsden, H. and Winter, J. (1994) 'Dorothy talks', interview in *Women and Theatre: Occasional Papers*, 2: 114–33.

Rea, C. (1972) 'Women's theatre groups', *The Drama Review*, 16 (2): 79–89.

—— (1974) 'Women for women', *The Drama Review*, 18 (4): 77–87.

Reinelt, J. (1994) *After Brecht: British Epic Theater*, Ann Arbor: University of Michigan Press.

Ricciardelli, S. (1992) 'Seen from the Moon', *Magdalena Newsletter*, 8: 3.

Ritchie, R. (ed.) (1987) *The Joint Stock Book: The Making of a Theatre Collective*, London: Methuen.

Robson, C., Georgeson, V. and Beck, J. (eds) (1990) *The Women Writers' Handbook*, London: Aurora Metro.

Rose, M. (1995) *Monologue Plays for Female Voices*, Torino: Tirrenia Stampatori.

Rudet, J. (1986) 'Afterword' to *Money to Live*, in M. Remnant (ed.) *Plays by Women: Volume Five*, London and New York: Methuen, p. 180.

Rutter, C. and Evans, F. (eds) (1988) *Clamorous Voices: Shakespeare's Women Today*, London: The Women's Press.

Schroeder, P.A. (1996) *The Feminist Possibilities of Dramatic Realism*, London: Associated University Presses.

Screen (1992) *The Sexual Subject: A Screen Reader in Sexuality*, London and New York: Routledge.

Showalter, E. (1987 [1985]) *The Female Malady*, London: Virago.

Siren (1997) 'Interview', in E. Aston (ed.) *Feminist Theatre Voices*, Loughborough: Loughborough Theatre Texts, pp. 77–101.

Solomon, A. (1997) *Re-Dressing the Canon: Essays on Theater and Gender*, London and New York: Routledge.

Spare Tyre (1997) 'Interview', in E. Aston (ed.) *Feminist Theatre Voices*, Loughborough: Loughborough Theatre Texts, pp. 102–24.

Spence, J. (1995) *Cultural Sniping: The Art of Transgression*, London and New York: Routledge.

Stanley, L. (1992) *The Auto/biographical I*, Manchester: Manchester University Press.

Stowell, S. (1992a) *A Stage of Their Own: Feminist Playwrights of the Suffrage Era*, Manchester: Manchester University Press.

—— (1992b) 'Rehabilitating realism', *Journal of Dramatic Theory and Criticism*, 6 (2): 81–8.

Strachey, M. (1912) 'Review of *Rutherford and Son*', *Englishwoman*, 14: 217–21.

Suzman, J. (1980) '*Hedda Gabler*: the play in performance', in E. Durbach (ed.) *Ibsen and the Theatre*, London: Macmillan, pp. 83–104.

Swindells, J. (1995) (ed.) *The Uses of Autobiography*, London: Taylor & Francis.

Todd, J. (n.d.) 'The playwright and the actress', in *The Glass Ceiling*, London: The Sphinx.

Wandor, W. (1979) 'Free collective bargaining', *Time Out*, 30 March–5 April, pp. 14–16.

—— (1983) 'Behind the fringe', interviews with Monstrous Regiment and Mrs Worthington's Daughters, *Plays and Players*, June, pp. 20–22.

Warner, D. (1996) 'Exploring space at play: the making of the theatrical event', *New Theatre Quarterly*, 13: 229–36.

Werner, S. (1996) 'Performing Shakespeare: voice training and the feminist actor', *New Theatre Quarterly*, 47: 249–58.

Williamson, J. (1983) 'Images of woman', *Screen*, 24: 102–16.

Women and Theatre (1997) 'Interview', in E. Aston (ed.) *Feminist Theatre Voices*, Loughborough: Loughborough Theatre Texts, pp. 125–41.

Women's Theatre Group (1997) 'Interview', in E. Aston (ed.) *Feminist Theatre Voices*, Loughborough: Loughborough Theatre Texts, pp. 33–51.

Zeig, S. (1985) 'The actor as activator: deconstructing gender through gesture', *Women and Performance*, 2 (2): 12–17.

Zivanovic, J. (1989) 'The rhetorical and political foundations of Women's Collaborative Theatre', in J. Redmond (ed.) *Themes in Drama: Women in Theatre: Volume 11*, Cambridge: Cambridge University Press, pp. 209–19.

Unpublished sources

Ankers, S. (1997) 'Response to Kathryn Hunter's Lear', post-production commentary, Loughborough University.

Greene, J. (1996) 'Analysis of *Imaging the Link*', Loughborough University.

Healey, E. (1997) 'Analysis of *Self-ish*', Loughborough University.

Jevons, S. (1996) 'Analysis of *Imaging the Link*', Loughborough University.

Savage, T. (1996) 'Analysis of *Imaging the Link*', Loughborough University.

Index